MW00532860

PRAISE FOR *THE HIVEMIND SWARMED*

"David Wolinsky doesn't just contend with where the internet has been and where it's going; he wades into the hell-swamps of Gamergate to do it, guided by sharp analysis from dozens of lively and thoughtful experts. . . . Remarkably timely . . . An essential document."

—STEPHEN THOMPSON, cohost of NPR's *Pop Culture Happy Hour*

"Brings together a who's who of game designers, journalists, industry insiders, academics, and players to constitute a modern-day Greek chorus for a sprawling, complexly layered, always engaging conversation about contemporary games culture. Essential reading."

—HENRY JENKINS, author of *Convergence Culture: Where Old and New Media Collide*

"David Wolinsky assembles a conversation that situates Gamergate within a nuanced, complex societal framework temporally spanning the dawn of personal computing to the present. . . . His volume is incredibly powerful, and a holistic and much-needed perspective on the impact of internet culture on all facets of our society."

—JACOB MCMURRAY, Museum of Pop Culture director of Curatorial, Collections, and Exhibits

"If you, like me, blinked and missed Gamergate, Wolinsky's oral history work is a refreshing window into a quickly moving and yet already historical target. . . . Multiple viewpoints, vivid longitudinal context, and poignant reflections leave us pondering the impact of digital discourse on our past, present, and future."

—JEN CRAMER, director, LSU Libraries Williams Center for Oral History

"Interviewing is an art form, and Wolinsky's prodigious skill draws out a never-before-seen web of complex personal truths surrounding events in the secretive and insular world of videogames that predict massive cultural events that follow, from Brexit to the 2016 US election and the global acceleration of nationalism."

—ERIN DRAKE KAJIOKA, *EA Spouse* blogger and head of Applied Game Design, Google Research

"An indispensable oral history of a crucial moment . . . A fascinating kaleidoscope of opinions that will be incredibly valuable to anyone looking back on these troubled times."

—RAPH KOSTER, author of *A Theory of Fun for Game Design*

"David Wolinsky has here gathered a diverse range of voices from witnesses and participants on the frontlines. When taken together, their testimonies form a compelling snapshot of a moment whose effects continue to affect an entire industry and its zealous fandoms."

—SIMON PARKIN, author of *A Game of Birds and Wolves: The Ingenious Young Women Whose Secret Board Game Helped Win World War II*

"With great agility, David Wolinsky provides critical conversations and insight from a rich cross section of people. . . . This is a wonderfully rare distillation of opinion, perspective, and comment on some of the most relevant forces shaping our society today."

—JEFFREY O. G. OGBAR, author of *Hip-Hop Revolution: The Culture and Politics of Rap*

"A riveting conversation . . . This book tells us that we need to talk more about blame, responsibility, and behavior as issues for the adults who make, play, and write about games."

—HENRY LOWOOD, curator for History of Science & Technology Collections and Film & Media Collections, Stanford University Libraries

THE
HIVEMIND
SWARMED

THE
HIVEMIND
SWARMED

CONVERSATIONS ON GAMERGATE, THE AFTERMATH, AND THE QUEST FOR A SAFER INTERNET

DAVID WOLINSKY

BEACON PRESS, BOSTON

BEACON PRESS
Boston, Massachusetts
www.beacon.org

Beacon Press books
are published under the auspices of
the Unitarian Universalist Association of Congregations.

27 26 25 24   8 7 6 5 4 3 2 1

This book is printed on acid-free paper that meets the uncoated paper
ANSI/NISO specifications for permanence as revised in 1992.

Text design and composition by Kim Arney

Library of Congress Cataloging-in-Publication Data is available for this title.
ISBN: 978-0-8070-1773-9; e-book: 978-0-8070-1772-2
audiobook: 978-0-8070-1771-5

CONTENTS

INTRODUCTION

> Safety is a story. . . . Beware of each other, because everything's about to change. The world is going to crack wide open. There is something on the horizon. A massive connectivity. The barriers between us will disappear, and we're not ready.
>
> —*Halt and Catch Fire*, season 3, episode 8: "You Are Not Safe," October 2016

THE TAKEAWAYS FROM GAMERGATE are hard to pin down. Today, just as in August 2014—when the movement's first coordinated online attacks against women exploded across Twitter under the hashtag #gamergate—the casualties and the stakes can only be explained in a clothesline of run-on sentences to people who either couldn't care less or couldn't care about anything else. As a harassment campaign that ignited quickly, spread even faster, and blocked the exits, it was the first undeniable warning that there might be something horribly wrong with our current incarnation of the internet. Rather than broaden our horizons and enable the exchange of ideas, the internet, post-Gamergate, seems destined to separate us into spaces that reinforce what we already believe. In these suffocating bubbles, we reject nuance and fight anyone who dares oppose us. A decade later, it remains pretty much impossible to convey how, in real-time, Gamergate scorched the earth of social media, leaving the soil there far more inhospitable to anything nourishing.

The details of Gamergate continue to be very, very challenging to explain or understand, and the reasons for this are straightforward. As a movement, it was designed to be that way and benefited from being chaotically copiloted by groups of smart, devious people who took things that were already true about the internet and leveraged them. Death threats, rape threats, and targeted extreme bad-faith arguments suddenly became a routine minute-by-minute reality. All the while, those who dogpiled to make things worse for whoever was unlucky enough to be targeted or those who tried to counterattack or de-escalate ultimately got sucked into what felt like a never-ending real-life online version of the Spider-Man Pointing meme. For the agitators, this aspect of Gamergate was a feature, not a bug—all the improbable details, mental forks in the road, and crazy-making migraines in holding many pointed but still muddled improbable details in your mind simultaneously were baked in.

Some background may help at least in offering a footing, though. In 2014, Gamergate was one of two things: either a widespread harassment campaign against women or, actually, about addressing corruption in videogame journalism. Really, part of the problem of making heads or tails of Gamergate was the way troll logic and conspiracy theories blasted enough gale-force winds to trick a lot of people into thinking the semantics mattered enough to ignore the bigger picture.

There was a lot of arguing—primarily on Twitter but also on Reddit,* YouTube, 4chan† boards, gaming websites, and blogs—about which of the two was the false flag and who was to blame. Mainly, everyone involved was addicted to picking fights. It was fucking horrible.

Here's how it started: In early August 2014, software developer Eron Gjoni, hurt by a messy breakup with game developer Zoë Quinn, published a nine-thousand-word "post about an ex" on the "Cringe-Worthy

---

* Unlike 4chan's much more minimal approach to moderation (see below), Reddit's message boards tend to be more actively moderated.

† Described on its official website as a "simple image-based bulletin board where anyone can post comments and share images" anonymously, 4chan has a complicated and anything-goes reputation. As Caitlin Dewey wrote for the *Washington Post* in October 2014, after Gamergate began, beyond 4chan serving as "the original incubator for a huge number of memes and behaviors that we now consider central to internet culture," it has also been a source of large-scale hoaxes, cyberbullying, and internet pranks. Simultaneously, it has served as a haven for hacktivists, being the birthplace of the collective Anonymous. Created by a fifteen-year-old Christopher "moot" Poole in 2003, the site has become synonymous with controversy due to its lax moderation policies. Dewey wrote that Poole "has argued convincingly that there's inherent value in having, and shedding, multiple identities online."

Break Up Stories" forum threads to *Something Awful** and *Penny Arcade*.[†] In his post, he accused Quinn of cheating on him with multiple journalists and one videogame critic, exchanging sex for favorable coverage and reviews of their[‡] games. Both forums deleted the post and reportedly banned Gjoni—exactly why remains uncertain and now is buried by the internet—so on August 16 he self-published the post to WordPress. From there, it spread to multiple boards on 4chan. In the months that followed, Gjoni's accusations—which, though swiftly debunked, nonetheless continued to linger—gained traction at further outposts including Reddit, *The Escapist*,[§] and GitHub.[¶]

This led to other writers, editors, and critics in the gaming space being accused of conflicts of interest with videogame developers. The fact that these claims were never substantiated didn't matter. As in all fandoms, every deeply angry gamer had critics they hated for writing "wrong" reviews. But what sets gaming apart is how far this resentment can be taken—many disgruntled fans craft conspiracy theories for why these reviews were written. When these additional accusations started circulating, more fans with similar grudges mobilized. Out came the pitchforks. The hivemind swarmed. Rallying under the hashtag #gamergate, bad actors seized on the groundless "conflict of interest" arguments and built a vicious movement that they claimed was dedicated to exposing journalistic corruption.

---

* *Something Awful*, founded in 1999, is a humor website that also hosts paywalled Web 1.0–style forums, where posters maintain a semi-anonymous identity. Its forums gave rise to a certain strain of internet humor, birthed into Weird Twitter—nihilistic, surreal, anti-humor—and in the early aughts it was generally the place to go to stay up on internet culture.

† *Penny Arcade* is a gaming-focused triweekly web comic with sometimes juvenile humor that has amassed a huge community and active forum around it. *Penny Arcade* also created a charity that has donated tons of money to children's hospitals and has spawned a convention, PAX, that meets three times a year.

‡ In January 2017, Quinn came out as non-cisgender and now prefers they/them pronouns.

§ An online gaming magazine, founded in 2005 and the original host site of the biting, wry animated videogame review series Zero Punctuation, narrated by British videogame developer Ben "Yahtzee" Croshaw.

¶ GitHub is a popular coding and collaboration platform geared toward software developers. Members on projects can also have threaded conversations with one another.

Gamergate had no leaders and no manifesto. People who got involved in Gamergate attacked women, minorities, and progressives who professionally created or criticized videogames, publicly sending them round-the-clock death and rape threats on Twitter and other social media platforms. After Quinn, the feminist media critic Anita Sarkeesian and the game developer Brianna Wu became Gamergate's main targets by August and September 2014, respectively. When perpetrators were called out for targeting women, they insisted, no, their crusade was advocating for more "ethical" coverage of videogames. But this is one of many confusing parts about the whole thing: there were people who said that sincerely and weren't threatening anyone, and there were other people who said that insincerely and *were* provoking confrontations wherever possible. A fleet of false flags provides ample cloud cover.

For months, in any online space where Gamergate's targets spoke or were spoken of, online or off, firehose bursts of hate followed in the form of crowdsourced public posts that routinely featured character assassination and explicit threats. Just a few such tweets, archived in the Wayback Machine's Twitter collection ethicsingamejournalism .com, read:

> "The search is on. AVFM is seeking to interview a gaming journalist that Zoe Quinn hasn't fucked. #GamerGate" —Paul Elam (@AVoiceForMen), September 19, 2014

> "A good woman is a great person. . . . An ignorant/victimizing feminist is a dumb cunt. #gamergate." —TechWarriorz (@tech warriorz), October 26, 2014

> "@MHPshow @femfreq Stop promoting your bullshit baseless views and you wont be harassed you fucking cunt!" —richard cranium (@richardcranium_), October 22, 2014

> "Always remember how #GamerGate started: a whore banged people to promote her video game" —Mark Fox (@swiftfox mark2), October 24, 2014

Through social media, gaming forums, gaming websites, and also anonymous image boards, many women's personal, and sometimes private, information was made public to incite further attacks. Some of these women risked their jobs or professional reputations by publicly responding to the attacks* while others, fearing for their safety, fled their homes.

By October that year, these cycles of argumentative violence within the movement caught former Kickstarter CTO Andy Baio's curiosity. As Gamergate continued to torture and roar, Baio wrote for Medium's *The Message*: "I've been using Twitter for eight years, but I've never seen behavior quite like this." Gamergate was so outside the norm, Baio had an impulse to leverage his programming know-how—coping skills distinctly available to technologists—to gather data to help himself and others make sense of what was happening. Baio wrote a program that captured all Gamergate activity on Twitter for seventy-two hours. From October 21 to 23, he found that there were 316,669 tweets from 38,630 accounts about Gamergate.

Is that a lot? Several months before Gamergate, in an April 2014 article, *PC Magazine* had attempted to compile a Twitter census—a task made challenging by the company's refusal to confirm "specific numbers of new user retention." The magazine found that an estimated 974 million accounts existed at the time. Approximately 44 percent of these accounts had never sent a single tweet, leaving around 550 million people who had tweeted within the previous twelve months. Only 126 million had sent tweets in the thirty days prior to the article's publication.

It's tempting to conclude that, based on the numbers, the attacks were being doled out by a few against a few. But if you're being targeted, the number of people attacking you doesn't really matter. Such a conclusion also overlooks the fact that by the time Gamergate happened, the world of videogames already had a long history—a

---

* As I came to learn later through my interviewing (and as you'll soon read), some videogame companies had, and continue to enforce, unwritten or explicitly spoken policies prohibiting workers from responding to these types of attacks. For example, in March 2016, Nintendo fired marketing specialist Alison Rapp for being the target of a sustained internet harassment campaign, though it insisted her termination was unrelated to "her being the subject of criticism from certain groups via social media several weeks ago," according to *Wired* (Julie Muncy, "Nintendo Firing a Female Gamer Only Makes the Trolls More Rabid," April 2016).

tradition—of dismissing any women who spoke out against sexism as "prudes" or "killjoys." During Gamergate, many women and marginalized people understood what was really going on: when it comes to online harassment verging into terrorism, we are living in a society without accountability. The trolls at 4chan leveraged the Rashomon effect to turn legions of gamers into *Manchurian Candidate*–style sleeper cells. One group's push for structural change became another's entertainment.

A 10-point type, 3,756-page Internet Relay Chat log documents a 4channer chatroom in which, from August 18 to September 6, Gamergate was plotted nearly 24/7 as a series of smoke screens designed to frustrate, gaslight, and intimidate Quinn and anyone who dared stand up for them. Here are a few moments:

> **<sarahv>**The problem is that making it about Zoe sleeping around amounts to a personal attack which, while funny and something she totally deserves, will hurt our chances of pushing the other point. . . .
>
> **<rd0951>**./v should be focused on the implications of gaming journalism. . . .
>
> **<sarahv>**Because SJWs will cherry-pick the /b/ shit posting and say "See? It's sexist MRAs!" . . .
>
> **<0pfag>**I'm debating whether or not we should just attack zoe. . . . push her . . . push her further. . . . . further, until eventually she an heroes . . .
>
> **<OtherGentleman>**What makes you think she has the balls to kill herself?
>
> **<0pfag>**I kind of want to just make her life irrepairably horrible. . . .
>
> **<NASA_Agent>**but what if she suicides. . . .
>
> **<0pfag>**Good. . . . Then we get to troll #RememberZoë

Throughout this log, Quinn's name appears 4,778 times (or roughly once a page)—mainly in gleeful messages fantasizing how to ruin their career, rape and kill them, or drive them to suicide. The word "journalism" appears 619 times.

While we're getting into the background on everything, now might be a good time to tell you a little about myself too. Apart from this introduction and the afterword, I've tried to put together this oral history on Gamergate's aftermath in a way so that what it's really about is up to you. I wanted to report and take the role of a messenger. I want you to draw your own conclusions. My fingerprints are in this book, but my voice isn't.

I'm someone who grew up in the 1980s, first watching over my brother's shoulder as he played computer games like *Police Quest* and *The Secret of Monkey Island* and, later, *Super Mario Bros 3*. In 1995, I became Hazel Crest, Illinois's Blockbuster Video store champion at *Donkey Kong Country*. I did not have some religious awakening the first time I touched a Nintendo controller. I am not approaching this book in defense of videogames or to invite you to play *Super Metroid*. I'm just someone who watched, horrified, as Gamergate began and started searching for understanding as others around me who were also watching—or were directly threatened—shut down.

To say that, at the time, Gamergate was disillusioning for me would not be quite accurate. I had recently moved from Chicago to Los Angeles, seeking stabler work outside the unstable world of journalism. After ten years of working in entertainment journalism that also included covering videogames (and once interviewing the comedian Gallagher), LA gave me my first opportunities to meet fellow critics IRL. Just before Gamergate hit, I had cultivated a growing group of new friends and colleagues looking to discuss the usual existential angst of a professional life covering hype cycles in TV, movies, literature, restaurants, and games—are we really *helping* anyone? I also had an ad hoc Twitter circle of fellow gaming outsiders and contrarian thinkers. We were a scattered, small bunch of people already looking for change, wanting to get people to think more and differently about videogames and about criticism in general. When Gamergate erupted, it felt like a confirmation of something many of us had sensed around the culture of videogames for forever—it had just never been given a name. Mainly, you tried to ignore it. Finally, I no longer could.

You don't need to have grown up playing videogames to see a way into understanding why Gamergate matters. It has relevance to anyone who wants to think about the systems we live in, about abuses of power in entertainment industries, about life in the trenches of tech industries, about propaganda, and about hope for healing. I'm someone who is *still* searching for understanding, and who takes comfort in the acceptance of a complicated, almost unknowable world. Also understand that I don't expect you to be like that.

A simple way to frame all the hurt that will be discussed by others in the pages ahead is that, while Gamergate affected a large number of people, the central communities involved have not had the opportunity to process it. Or they understandably don't want to think about the trauma again.

Gamergate holds the grim distinction of codifying the modern online harassment campaign. It cemented new tactics for future culture wars by weaponizing one of the internet's greatest drawbacks/features: the ability to hurt each other in new ways, via new channels. Provided you've already invested time into assembling the right kind of network—and recognize your peer group's potential to rally against a common enemy, no questions asked—you can run ops as complex, confounding, and effective as the KGB's.

Trying to find meaning in Gamergate's aftermath beyond that is tricky. In the gaming world, it has metastasized from the thing that shall not be named to the thing we talk about all the time without talking about it. Those who watched the initial attacks felt powerless, paralyzed, and eventually exhausted. We lurked and silently observed as bands of activists and vigilantes rose to challenge blatant misogyny and conspiracy theories. Those who looked away from Gamergate, or never heard of it, missed the experience of witnessing the movement's demonstration that the digital and physical worlds are intertwined.

The media initially largely ignored the whole ugly ordeal and its destructive spiral, largely weighing in to hastily, bluntly blur the facts or finger-wag in paragraphs that boiled down to, "Well, what'd you expect? Gamers have always been *toxic*."

I accept that this perception exists and is not likely to go out of circulation anytime soon—and maybe it doesn't deserve to. But many of the unhealthy dynamics that exist in gaming can also be found in pretty much every other activity that brings people together. On Reddit, there's a forum called r/HobbyDrama* dedicated exclusively to documenting and discussing "meaningful controversy" that "might have ousted someone from [a] community, shaped perception of the hobby, altered the rules of hobby uses, divided the community, created a new faction, caused significant outrage, etc." Scrolling through May 2023 to January 2024—when I'm writing this—and stopping randomly, tales emerge of vicious rivalries in the fandoms of figure skating, *Who Wants to Be a Millionaire?*, Formula One racing, and chick lit. The subreddit's icon is a flaming ball of yarn, impaled by a pair of knitting needles.

But Gamergate was unusual in that it ensnared fan communities, trolls, *and* the global workforce of videogames (which spans countless disciplines and areas of expertise, companies ranging anywhere from six to ten-thousand-plus people, publishers, publicists, hardware manufacturers, engine developers, and on and on), plus the gaming media (an international landscape that includes major outlets, fan blogs, forums, YouTube, review aggregators, industry news and analysis sites, and on and on). None of these are monoliths.

As years have passed and further traumas—insert your favorite least favorite current event here, online or off—have stacked to numb everyone, what we've all missed is a chance to make sense of Gamergate. *The Hivemind Swarmed* is a portrayal of all the psychic damage wrapped up in it.

This is a thread I've been pulling on for a long time, and not alone. In 2014 I founded Don't Die, an interview series that has sought to chronicle Gamergate as it was scorching daily. I wanted to create a kind of online lighthouse for the lost—a place to explore questions that I felt weren't being asked. These conversations have provided a space for people who were moved to reflect and readers to mourn what and who we lost during Gamergate. They have also been an opportunity for me to listen to other frontline witnesses and people from other

---

* On Reddit, communities are organized into subreddits, each designated with an "r/" followed by the topic. For example, "r/gaming" refers to the gaming community, where members share discussions and news related to gaming. In 2023, there were an estimated 3,125,000 total subreddits on Reddit.

subcultures who, in the past or recent present, were forced to look at aspects of Gamergate (such as how the worlds of architecture, restaurants, or YA publishing address sexism, etc.). I also got people deep in the gaming world past and present to speak about the industry's lack of ownership or regret over the "gamer" culture it helped to nurture.

The videogame industry is, as a rule, very guarded. Anything a worker does or learns while employed at a game company could be considered a trade secret. Gaming companies' and their workers' relationship with the press has always been very well-managed. I remember visiting one studio in April 2014 to write a game preview and sitting across from the team's senior designer and PR rep, asking whether the game I'd been assigned to cover would simulate both day- and nighttime lighting. After some anxious whispered conferring, they declined to comment—the implication being there was a fear of falsely getting up hopes among gamers, who would pounce if they felt they'd been promised one thing but delivered another.

The idea of asking industry people for introspection, for their honest reactions on what was happening with Gamergate, that type of openness, was rare until Don't Die. But this is what I've been up to for the last decade. However, despite my chronic curiosity and tenacity, I have to tell you going in that this book offers no pat answers. Because there aren't any.

Ten years later, Gamergate stands as something that most people I cross paths with scoff at when it's even mentioned. Many people in the gaming world don't want to talk about it. They see no upside to stepping back into the radiation field and actively avoid getting dragged into another conversation about it—especially with a stranger or some oral historian/author. If bringing it up in conversation is nauseating to anyone who watched it happen or lived through it, then seeing it on the spine of a book arouses suspicion. It's considered a closed topic, arid, without anything further to tell us about the world we live in today. But "we are done thinking about this" only slams doors.

I sympathize with those who feel sick just hearing the word "Gamergate." But the social internet has become such an integral part of so many people's lives that muting the topic passes up the opportunity to better understand how we talk to each other online, and how the internet changes conversations. We have to keep talking about it.

In arson cases, the fire department doesn't institutionally shrug its shoulders and say, "Well, what'd you expect? Houses have always been *flammable.*" Law enforcement is called in, investigators check the scene, samples are collected and analyzed. Witnesses are interviewed. Suspects are identified. If enough evidence is gathered, parties will be arrested, charged, and prosecuted. We prevent it from happening again.

The FBI did investigate certain aspects of Gamergate as it unfolded, extending into 2015. In 2017, the agency published a heavily redacted 173-page report (not counting 61 additional deleted pages) that ultimately led to no charges being filed. In the end, the FBI was unable to identify who was behind the threats, declined to prosecute additional individuals who were likely implicated or involved in some way, and generally ran into jurisdictional issues. In a culture of mayhem, where everywhere we look we're reminded we're on our own, safety is a story that we tell ourselves. But the atomic unit of a culture is its stories—which is why I remain curious and dedicated to listening.

Including more voices in making sense of a hate campaign—as this book tries to do—is the ground floor. It helps us all understand and navigate—and hopefully address—the unintended consequences of the careless systems that have come to define the internet as we know it. It also helps us remember that every individual affected by those systems *is* an individual. Awareness is a rope we pull on together. We can lift the curtain, or we can drag it the other way.

Before you read ahead, understand that in no way does this book pretend to be a definitive record of Gamergate. *The Hivemind Swarmed* is a patchwork quilt of conversations with a variety of people who were in and outside of Gamergate's first detonation. It's them talking about its effects and implications, about the time since and the road ahead. The narrators here, largely, are still trying to make sense of it. Many speak of redemption for the internet and for videogames as an industry and culture—they wonder whether that's still a possibility, something that's moment has passed, or maybe just a myth.

After years of following the conversational breadcrumbs with Don't Die, I wanted to take what I had been hearing and cast a holistic net to see how many people of varying distances to ground zero felt the explosion. This book contains the voices of videogame-industry pioneers, pinball-industry visionaries, early Silicon Valley thinkers, pop-culture essayists, musicians, academics, tech journalists, entertainment journalists, videogame-community managers, videogame publicists, videogame creative directors, cartoonists, HR professionals, cosplayers, authors, writers, people who have quit the videogame industry both recently and long ago, historians, TV critics, TV producers, activists, museum curators, technologists, teenagers, and filmmakers. This book also casts aside the common temptation to explain videogame culture by only looking at videogame culture. To really even begin to grapple with Gamergate, you have to invite the rest of the world—or the portions that are willing to discuss it, anyway—to the conversation. None of the perpetrators of Gamergate were interviewed for this book—they've had their say, and there are no good-faith discussions to be had. The movement was designed to flip any attempt at discussion into conflict.

But, if any Gamergate participant cares to speak to me in an open, honest, transparent, and verifiable way, I'm still around.

For readers who are already familiar with some of the events discussed in these pages, my aim was to go outside existing published narratives and arguments about them. This book comes at the story of Gamergate from a different direction, told by asking broader questions and, more pointedly, posing them to unexpected voices. Quinn, Wu, and Sarkeesian are noticeably—and intentionally—largely absent for this reason. As one of those women told me, their relationship with the topic is like "being in a band, and people want me to play the hits." They're trying to move on and, like the rest of us, process the whole nightmare.

—DAVID WOLINSKY
Chicago
January 2024

ORAL HISTORY METHODOLOGY

INTERVIEWS WERE CONDUCTED for this book between the summers of 2018 and 2019. Eighty-eight people sat and talked with me for a combined eighty-seven hours, forty-three minutes, and twenty-one seconds. This total doesn't count the additional time some generously gave for additional follow-ups for clarification over email.

These interviews were conducted in parallel to my interview series, Don't Die (2014–present), which lives at nodontdie.com. While all interviews for the book were done separately from the series and were never previously published online, the two undertakings have informed each other deeply. When I began work on this book, I took everything that I had learned with Don't Die and then burrowed down specifically on the questions that form the foundation of *The Hivemind Swarmed*. This book is the result of my alarmed curiosity, my desire to listen, and hundreds of conversations where the only goal was to get the narrators and myself off-script.

Where narrators have given consent, interview recordings for this book have been donated to the Silicon Valley Archives, Stanford University, and will be available to researchers in the David Wolinsky Papers.

Don't Die itself is also preserved by Stanford Libraries, with research that—including this book—spans 525 interviews across 612-plus hours of audio and counting. You can access this collection via Stanford's online library catalog at searchworks.stanford.edu/view/13768655. It benefits from the nearly two decades of momentum I gained from working as a documentary researcher and, before that, an editor for publications including *The Onion*, *A.V. Club*, and NBC, where my job was finding and reporting on artists and stories slipping through the cracks.

This continuum of work includes collaborations with the University of Washington's Information School, Carnegie Mellon University's Human-Computer Interaction Institute, Stanford University, and Northeastern University. These partnerships have helped to begin to grow the archive into a resource, from building out data dictionaries and metadata to exploring the use of AI in making the collection more accessible. (If you have skills in any of these or related areas, or think you might be able to help at all, please reach out—I'm "just" an interviewer.) I'm hoping that what started as a safe harbor for conversations digging into questions I felt were being largely unexplored in the media can become an impactful time capsule for future generations to understand what happened to us in the early twenty-first century, "reboot" the status quo, and pave a way to healing.

Until future generations shift the entrenched trends within the videogame world and open it up to more diversity, all accounts on the industry's ecosystem and history will be dominated by white men. While *The Hivemind Swarmed* is unable to change the past, attention was paid to amplifying under-represented voices.

In very rare cases, what people told me has been edited for clarity. In all cases, people's vocal tics and natural way of speaking is presented as-is—both to present individuals in their own words and to demonstrate how everyone's gears are still actively turning on these topics. To help you better understand the rules of the road in reading the pages ahead: Ellipses have been inserted to punctuate sentences where the speaker interrupts themselves or there are omissions, with long dashes standing in to convey interruptions or asides. Where excerpts from real-time text-based communication from the internet have been included, chat logs and exchanges are presented verbatim.

NARRATORS

THE OPINIONS EXPRESSED in this book are those of the contributors and do not represent the opinions of their employers. Each contributor's listed professional title relates to their relevant experience with the themes raised in this book and does not indicate their occupation at the time of publication.

ALBA
Videogame streamer

During the writing of this book, Alba reached out, wanting to share her story of being drugged at an in-person videogame competition in 2015 and of how her subsequent attempts to speak out were, as she said, "written off" as "not that big of a deal."

SHANNON APPELCLINE
Role-playing-game historian

Editor in chief and admin of RPGnet, which introduces itself as "the oldest and largest independent role-playing [game] site on the internet," and the author of *Designers & Dragons*, a four-volume history of the role-playing industry.

WAGNER JAMES AU
Journalist/Second Life historian

Author of *The Making of Second Life*, a 2009 book chronicling his time working as an embedded journalist in the online virtual world for Linden Labs, the internet company and software developer of Second Life.

RICHARD BARTLE
Online game pioneer/researcher

Co-creator of MUD1 (1978), perhaps the oldest virtual world in existence. In 2000, Bartle published a study classifying behavior in online videogame players.

REVA BASCH
Women on The WELL conference host

Moderator, from 1990 to 1995, of a protected message board exclusive to female members on The WELL, one of the oldest internet communities.

VANGIE BEAL
GameGirlz founder

GameGirlz (1997–2007) was billed as a women's games and tech site, and in addition to features, previews, and reviews it regularly published spotlight profiles of women in the industry to encourage inclusion. Many game companies approached Beal for advice on how to better reach girls and cater to their gaming tastes.

AARON BLEYAERT
Conan senior digital producer

Late-night TV host Conan O'Brien's "assistant nerd" and the driving force behind its popular "Clueless Gamer" segments.

IAN BOGOST
Atlantic writer/videogame developer

Author of *How to Talk About Videogames* (2015) and *Persuasive Games: The Expressive Power of Videogames* (2010). Frequently writes about play and how tech is changing humanity and vice versa.

SERAPHINA BRENNAN
Warner Bros. Games community manager

Writer, producer, and online community manager for more than a decade. Also worked at Trion Worlds.

ANGELINA BURNETT
Halt and Catch Fire writer

Activist and community organizer, currently on the Writers Guild of America's board of directors. She was a co-executive producer and writer on *Halt and Catch Fire*, a period TV drama whose four seasons document the personalities and ideals behind the US home-computing invasion and, later, the internet.

NOLAN BUSHNELL
Atari cofounder

Cofounder of Atari, the company that planted the flag for the modern commercial arcade and videogame industries. Atari, established in 1972, helped set the norms for the videogame industry and videogame culture in the West. Remember *Pong*? *Asteroids*? *Centipede*? All Atari.

LINDA CARLSON
Sony Online Entertainment community manager

Customer-experience executive and consultant who has also managed communities at Trion Worlds.

HEATHER CHAPLIN
Author/media critic

Co-author of *Smartbomb*, a 2006 travelogue of the videogame industry and culture as it looked that year. The book also profiles many influential figures and personalities weighing in on issues important to videogames then, and rippling into today.

HOWARD CHAYKIN
Cartoonist

Artist and writer perhaps best known for his 1980 sci-fi and satire comic-book series *American Flagg!*

KUKHEE CHOO
Media studies professor

Former comic-book artist, television producer, and film-production assistant who now teaches courses about race and gender, popular culture, and the history of media technology. At Tokyo's Sophia University, she researches globalization and feminism.

JONATHAN COULTON
Musician

Performer known for writing songs about outcasts who are trying to make sense of the worlds that shun them. From 2018 until 2022, TV's *The Good Fight* featured a steady stream of *Schoolhouse Rock!*–like peppy primers from Coulton, each one a topical look at of-the-moment subjects like internet trolls and cultural appropriation.

DAVID CROATTO
MAD magazine senior editor

From 1996 until 2016, Croatto served as *MAD* magazine's senior editor. Since the 1950s, *MAD*'s mission has been to teach young readers to cultivate a healthy skepticism of media, advertising, and authority.

JASON DEMARCO
Adult Swim senior vice president

Senior executive for Adult Swim, he has been with Cartoon Network since 1996. DeMarco is also the co-creator of the Toonami programming block showcasing anime, and he founded the network's Williams Street Records imprint, which frequently releases hip-hop compilations.

HARRY DENHOLM
No Man's Sky senior programmer

After the game's launch in 2017, Denholm announced his departure from the company on social media.

DAVID DEWALD
BioWare community manager

Helped build and maintain online communities in the years between 1998 and 2011 for IGN (*Planet Dungeon Siege*), Acclaim (*9Dragons*), and BioWare (*Star Wars: The Old Republic*).

KATIE FLEMING
Katie's Tomb Raider Site founder

Fleming's site is one of a handful thanked in the 2013 *Tomb Raider* reboot's credits. From 2000 through 2017, the site was a home for her fan fiction and game screenshots. The latter was unusual because other *Tomb Raider* fansites primarily focused on sharing official screenshots previously published by the developer. Fleming's work on the site ultimately led to employment in the game industry as a community manager.

BEN FRITZ
Wall Street Journal bureau chief

As a staff writer at *Variety* from 2004 to 2009, Fritz reported on the film business, corporate earnings, digital media, and—unusually for a respected and mainstream-facing publication at the time—videogames. Fritz has gone on to write *The Big Picture: The Fight for the Future of Movies* and has contributed to the *Los Angeles Times*.

PAUL GALLOWAY
MoMA NY collection specialist

Instrumental in adding videogames to New York's Museum of Modern Art collection in 2012.

GRACE
Fat, Ugly, or Slutty? cofounder

From 2011 to 2013, Grace and three of her friends ran *Fat, Ugly, or Slutty?*, an online archive of the rude, crude, and generally immature messages anonymous strangers send to female videogame players—usually on Xbox Live. Described on their site as "creepy, degrading, and funny," these anonymous messages are categorized under a dozen headings like "unprovoked rage," "death threats," and "crudely creative." Grace now works in the tech industry.

JENNY HANIVER
Not in the Kitchen Anymore founder

In 2000, Haniver started recording and posting online the random hostile and vulgar encounters she was having with male players in games like *Call of Duty*. These brief snippets, rarely longer than a minute and usually as short as fourteen seconds, catalogue what can be, for many women, the typical experience and trade-offs of playing online videogames.

GINA HARA
Filmmaker

Creative director of the Technoculture, Art, and Games Research Centre in Montréal. Hara is a Canadian-Hungarian filmmaker and artist whose 2017 documentary *Geek Girls* explores "the hidden half of fan culture: nerdy women."

STEPHANIE HARVEY
***Counter-Strike* world champion**

A five-time world champion in competitive *Counter-Strike*. Previously, Harvey worked as a game designer for Ubisoft Montréal on *Prince of Persia: The Forgotten Sands* and *Far Cry Primal*. Harvey is an advocate for promoting and creating awareness of gender equality, cyber dependence, and cyberbullying.

MIKE HILL
Videogame/film creative consultant

Hill has worked across TV, film, and videogames on productions including *Game of Thrones*, *Blade Runner 2049*, *Call of Duty: Infinite Warfare*, and *Horizon: Zero Dawn*.

ALEX HUTCHINSON
Ubisoft creative director

Creative director for Ubisoft on *Far Cry 4* and *Assassin's Creed 3* and also Electronic Arts on *Army of Two: The 40th Day*.

JOI ITO
MIT Media Lab director

Venture capitalist, entrepreneur, writer, and scholar focusing on the ethics and governance of technology. At the MIT Media Lab, Ito's work on technology centered on imagining, exploring, and building better uses for it.

EUGENE JARVIS
Atari programmer

An Atari employee in the late '70s. In the decades since, Jarvis has been designing pinball games, arcade games, and home videogames. Since 2001, Jarvis has been the president of his own game studio, Raw Thrills.

SOREN JOHNSON
Civilization IV **lead designer**

Videogame designer and programmer who worked for Firaxis Games from 2000 to 2007. Johnson helped design several of the company's other games, including *Dragon Age Legends* and *Spore*.

STEVE JONES
Internet researcher/professor

A University of Illinois at Chicago Distinguished Professor specializing in the cultural impact of new media platforms and devices. Online user since 1979, he is the founder and president of the Association of Internet Researchers.

BEVERLY KEEL
Change the Conversation cofounder

Middle Tennessee State University's chair of the Department of Recording Industry. Keel has been a professor at MTSU since 1995. She's also a former senior vice president for Universal Media Group and an award-winning music journalist and pop-culture commentator for *People*, VH1, and *Parade*. In 2014, Keel cofounded Change the Conversation, a coalition to help fight gender inequality in country music.

STEVE KENT
Journalist

In the '90s Kent became a columnist—and, in many cases, the only writer—who covered videogames for outlets including the *Seattle Times*, the Los Angeles Times Syndicate, the *Japan Times*, and MSNBC. He was active during a period of great expansion in and also great challenges to the industry. Kent was called upon to speak in the 1993–94 US Senate hearings about videogame violence and wrote the entries on videogames for *Encarta* and *Encyclopedia Americana*.

FLOURISH KLINK
Fanslaining cohost

Alongside journalist Elizabeth Minkel, the pair's *Fansplaining* podcast dives deep into the gnarled, intricate, and existential questions about what it means to be a fan—and often flips these questions to academics, writers, fan creators, and people from the entertainment industry.

CHUCK KLOSTERMAN
Author/pop-culture essayist

Essayist, columnist, and journalist who dissects pop culture. Klosterman is known for weighing in on videogames in his 2006 *Esquire* essay, "The Lester Bangs of Videogames," which invoked Lester Bangs, a prominent rock music critic, and Pauline Kael, a celebrated film critic, in service of Klosterman's growing suspicions "that there will never be that kind of authoritative critical voice within the world of videogames."

LORA KOLODNY
CNBC.com tech reporter

Covers start-ups, regulatory issues impacting tech companies, and emerging industries for CNBC.com.

CHRIS KRAMER
Videogame publicist

Kramer has managed or been involved with all aspects of outbound communication for major videogame companies and firms including Capcom, Tencent America, Sony Online Entertainment, and Forty-seven Communications.

DAVID KUSHNER
Journalist/*Masters of Doom* author

Rolling Stone contributing editor. He has also written articles for the *New Yorker*, *Vanity Fair*, and *GQ*. Most relevantly to the videogame world, Kushner has written behind-the-curtain biographies on the creative teams behind *Doom* in 2004 (*Masters of Doom*) and *Grand Theft Auto* in 2012 (*Jacked*).

LULU LAMER
Videogame producer

LaMer started in the videogame industry in 1998 as an associate producer for Looking Glass Studios for titles including *Thief: The Dark Project* and *System Shock*, and she worked her way up to senior producer at 2K in 2008 for titles including *Spec Ops: The Line* and *Borderlands*. In 2016, LaMer became the director of studio development for Funomena. LaMer quit the videogame industry in 2017.

BRENDA LAUREL
Purple Moon cofounder

An Atari employee in the early '80s. In the late '90s, Laurel went on to become cofounder and VP of design at Purple Moon, which led research on and created games for girls. Wildly popular, Purple Moon's *Rockett's New School* outsold *John Madden Football* in 1997.

JON LEBKOWSKY
Writer/early internet activist

Early online network advocate and activist. An early adopter, Lebkowsky was a member of The WELL, back when the internet was only text. Lebkowsky was also a crusader for e-commerce's potential (helping Whole Foods internally embrace the internet in 1997) and for a free and open internet (cofounding the Electronic Frontier Foundation's Austin, Texas, chapter in 1990).

TIM LONGO
***Halo* creative director**

Longo has been in the videogame industry since 1997 and has worked for LucasArts, Crystal Dynamics, and 343 Industries. Longo was the creative director for the *Tomb Raider* reboot (2013), *Halo 5: Guardians* (2015), and *Halo Infinite* (2021).

AL LOWE
***Leisure Suit Larry* creator**

Lowe's name is synonymous with the late-'80s to mid-'90s campy computer-game series *Leisure Suit Larry*. Lowe wrote, designed, and programmed all six of the Sierra On-Line *Leisure Suit Larry* titles, which are about a hapless and sleazy loser desperately trying to get laid.

CHRIS MANCIL
Electronic Arts global director of community

In addition to his role with Electronic Arts—the second-largest gaming company in terms of revenue during his tenure—Mancil has worked as THQ's director of digital and social media, Trion Worlds' director of community management, and Sierra On-Line's senior manager of community relations. He has worked in the videogame industry since 1999.

JASON MANNING
Author/sociologist

In 2014, Manning (an associate professor in West Virginia University's Sociology and Anthropology Department) and his colleague Bradley Campbell (an associate professor of sociology at California State University at Los Angeles) published a paper about a new moral code in American life: "victimhood culture," where people have a heightened sensitivity to slights and seek recourse by publicizing their own victimhood. The paper was expanded into the 2018 book *The Rise of Victimhood Culture: Microaggressions, Safe Spaces, and the New Culture Wars*.

BRIAN MCCULLOUGH
Internet historian

Author of the 2018 book *How the Internet Happened: From Netscape to the iPhone*. McCullough is also the host of the *Internet History Podcast*, which features interviews with people who were in the room for landmark moments that shaped the internet as we know it today.

AMERICAN MCGEE
Doom designer

A Shanghai-based videogame developer, McGee has worked in the industry for nearly three decades, starting in 1993 as a level designer for *Doom* and other later id Software titles.

BETHANY MCLEAN
Fortune editor at large

McLean is the coauthor, as she describes in her official bio, "of several books on business gone wrong," including *The Smartest Guys in the Room: The Amazing Rise and Scandalous Fall of Enron* (2004) and *All the Devils Are Here: The Hidden History of the Financial Crisis* (2011). In 2005, McLean published the *Fortune* article "Sex, Lies, and Videogames" about Rockstar Games' "financial chicanery" that asked, "Why don't investors care?"

JOANNE MCNEIL
Art critic/writer

McNeil frequently publishes essays and other projects about human expression and technology, including the 2018 web series *Just Browsing*. In 2020, McNeil dug deeper on these themes in the book *Lurking: How a Person Became a User*.

RON MEINERS
The Sims 3 community manager

According to his LinkedIn profile, Meiners has worked with videogame communities since 1996 with a focus on, and belief in, "working with unhappy communities to turn them around and into brand loyalists." Meiners's experience in that field also includes working as community manager for *Tom Clancy's Splinter Cell: Chaos Theory*.

CLARINDA MERRIPEN
Videogame operations director

From 1997 to 2005, Merripen oversaw human resources departments at Cyberlore Studios and then Cryptic Studios. In the years since, she has shifted to consulting for tech and game companies on corporate-culture issues.

LAURA MILLER
Salon cofounder/literary critic

Journalist who writes for the *New Yorker*, *Harper's Magazine*, and *The Guardian*. *Don't Starve* and *Don't Starve Together* aficionado with a combined playtime of 5,866 hours logged.

MOBY
Musician

A songwriter, producer, and animal rights activist, Moby is widely recognized as a pioneering figure of electronic dance music. The video for his 2016 single "Are You Lost in the World Like Me?" depicts a bleak and dystopian world where people are completely immersed in their smartphones, oblivious to their surroundings and the people around them.

KATE MOSER
Nintendo copyeditor

From 2010 to 2013, Moser edited for Nintendo public-facing text on videogames, videogame systems, and manuals.

LISA NAKAMURA
Gender and technology researcher

A scholar examining race, gender, and sexuality in digital media. Nakamura's research and teachings on these subjects have informed several books, including her *Digitizing Race: Visual Cultures of the Internet* (2008).

EMILY NUSSBAUM
The New Yorker TV critic

In 2016, Nussbaum won a Pulitzer Prize for what the Pulitzer Prize Board praised as "television reviews written with an affection that never blunts the shrewdness of her analysis or the easy authority of her writing."

RUKMINI PANDE
Race and fandom researcher

Pande critiques fandom through a lens of racial, cultural, and ethnic identity. An assistant professor at O. P. Jindal Global University in Sonipat, India, Pande is also on the editorial board of the *Journal of Fandom Studies*.

RAJ PATEL
Author/labor activist

A writer whose work examines the intersection of food, agriculture, and politics, and who can regularly be read in *The Guardian*, Patel has published several books on these themes, including *Stuffed and Starved: The Hidden Battle for the World Food System* (2008).

ANDRÉS PERTIERRA
r/AskHistorians moderator
A historian specializing in Cuba and US-Cuban relations in the nineteenth and twentieth centuries, Pertierra moderates the AskHistorians subreddit, where members may ask questions or start discussions about history.

VENKATESH RAO
Writer/tech consultant
Rao consults with senior technology executives on hammering out better ideas and approaches for management in what he calls "sparring sessions." As a writer, he explores culture and how we should interact with each other, as exemplified in his 2018 essay titled "Pack Experience," which was published on his blog, *Ribbonfarm*.

HOWARD RHEINGOLD
Virtual community pioneer/writer
Prolific writer who has been thinking about digital culture's future since the internet's very beginning. Rheingold has been a constant presence in translating, advocating, and pondering how the online world is shaping the way we communicate with, and relate to, each other. His books include *Tools for Thought: The History and Future of Mind-Expanding Technology* (1985) and *Net Smart: How to Thrive Online* (2012).

MAUREEN RYAN
Variety TV critic
Television critic for the *New York Times*, the *Hollywood Reporter*, *Vulture*, *TV Guide*, and many others. From 2015 to 2019, Ryan was *Variety*'s chief TV critic.

RAWN SHAH
Playing MUDs on the Internet coauthor
Shah's 1995 book, cowritten with Jim Romine, is a strategy guide for finding, playing, and becoming an expert at early online multiplayer

games. Their book now doubles as a historical record of the online norms of yesteryear.

ROGER SHARPE
Pinball designer

Sharpe "saved" pinball. In 1976, his testimony and demonstration before the New York City Council showed the game was skill-based (previously, it had been considered luck-based and therefore gambling) reversing a thirty-four-year ban on pinball machines. He also wrote a 1977 book on pinball (*Pinball!*) and published many magazine articles during the era of videogames' arrival.

STEVE SPOHN
The AbleGamers Charity COO

Advocate for encouraging the game development world to be more inclusive of disabled individuals. In 2014, AbleGamers was targeted by Gamergate.

CLIVE THOMPSON
Wired contributing editor

Contributing writer for the *New York Times Magazine* and a monthly columnist for *Wired*. Thompson also writes a periodic column about the history of technology for *Smithsonian* magazine.

JENNIFER WADELLA
Fat, Ugly, or Slutty? cofounder

From 2011 to 2013, Wadella and three friends ran *Fat, Ugly, or Slutty?*, an online archive of the rude, crude, and generally immature messages anonymous strangers send to female videogame players.

RICH WEIL
FusionFall community manager

Managed online communities since 2004. From 2007 to 2009, Weil was the director of community relations for Cartoon Network's *FusionFall*, an online-enabled multiplayer game intended for younger players.

DAVID WEINBERGER
The Cluetrain Manifesto coauthor

In 1999, Weinberger and a few of his analyst, journalist, and consultant colleagues published *The Cluetrain Manifesto*, a set of ninety-five principles that signaled how companies needed to take more responsibility in their marketing and approach to representing themselves online. His other books include *Everything Is Miscellaneous: The Power of the New Digital Disorder* and *Everyday Chaos: Technology, Complexity, and How We're Thriving in a New World of Possibility*.

JOE WHITTAKER
Counterterrorism researcher

Research fellow at The Hague's International Centre for Counter-Terrorism, an independent think tank providing multidisciplinary policy advice on prevention and the rule of law. Whittaker has been researching how terrorist groups recruit using the internet.

MICHAEL WILSON
Cosplayer

An Ohio deputy sheriff, Wilson has been cosplaying at conferences and charity events since 2012.

KEN WONG
Monument Valley lead designer

A Melbourne, Australia-based artist, illustrator, and designer, Wong has worked on games including *Florence* (2018) and *Land's End* (2015).

DIXON WU
Neo Geo World Tour organizer

Hong Kong-based organizer of Neo Geo World Tour, a global videogame tournament.

The
HIVEMIND
SWARMED

CHAPTER 1

WTF IS GAMERGATE?

Excerpts from irc chatroom #burgersandfries created by 4channers, August 2014:

AUG 18 17.37.57

<SweetJBro>lol I'm tweeting Zoe's nudes to some of her defenders.

AUG 18 20.10.06

<nullspace>i couldnt care less about vidya, i just want to see zoe receive her comeuppance . . .

<yetsturdy>i want a social botnet . . .

yes

augmented trolling. :) . . .

<PEANESS>using neutral language processing to create realistic & generic SJW posts, creating reputations for many accounts . . . which is something that i specialize in

<nullspace>make it happen . . .

<PEANESS>i don't specialize in english very much

<yetsturdy>PEANESS: that first part is a little silly . . .

people will catch on to markov bots pretty quick

they can be used to maybe generate initial followers, but not for long-term psyops

<PEANESS>which is why it wouldn't be original content, mostly

<yetsturdy>if there were tools that made it really easy to manage many sockpuppet identities, then we'd have something good and better than sockpuppets: stolen accounts

<PEANESS>it would be old stuff from old bloggers, repurposed with
the words switched around

<yetsturdy>mind-control, in a very loose sense.

<platonicSolid>big dreams dude . . .

<PEANESS>if you're working with stolen accounts, you're working on
borrowed time . . .

they have their place, but if you're going to annhilation instead
of irritation then you need more

plus sjws have pretty strong friends groups that exist outside of
tumblr; account stealings will be caught onto quickly

AUG 19 02.28.30

<mugg>okay, is zoe actually depressed?

<kailasha>i bet she is now

<mugg>diagnosed etc?

<meshnetguy>kek . . .

<Opus>I think she tried killing herself before

<kailasha>she should try that again :^) . . .

AUG 21 17.49.45

<OtherGentleman>The more you try to attack her directly, the more
she gets to play the victim card and make a bunch of friends
who will support her because, since she has a vagina, any attack
is misgony

<rd0951>./v should be in charge of the gaming journalism aspect
of it. /pol should be in charge of the feminism aspect, and /b
should be in charge of harassing her into killing herself

AUG 21 23.20.35

<rd0951>there should be a massive campaign to tweet zoe her own
nudes . . .

<Silver|2>They've been tweeted at her a lot

AUG 25 03.10.37

<akiyuki_shinbo>wait what are we plotting

<sangria>i don't even know
but i like it . . .

MAUREEN RYAN, *Variety* **TV critic:**

If you look at the foundational document of Gamergate—Zoë Quinn's ex—it's abusive and it's mean and it's shitty, but what it foundationally is, is that "she betrayed me." What's the foundation of that betrayal? Turn on your radio someday and just take note of the percentage of songs that could be translated as: "She would no longer do my emotional work for me." And I'm not saying that we don't all ask that of each other, but honestly the dynamic of men being unable to process their emotions and their hurts and their injuries and their questions and their desires without having a woman there to do it for them or be either their carer or, whatever, therapist? That's a huge part of this. In the most reductive view, women are viewed as possessions to acquire. Those possessions will give you status, and then those possessions will also do your work for you. And if those conditions aren't met, then what are women for? So there's this foundational misogyny that they decided to just go all in on.

AARON BLEYAERT, *Conan* **senior digital producer:**

Yeah, you know what? Run down Gamergate for me in a nutshell. What that was?

CHUCK KLOSTERMAN, **author/pop-culture essayist:**

I don't even know if I know exactly what happened, to be honest. To say I followed it, it's like, I saw that hashtag used a lot. I saw a lot of people expressing outrage over it. I know that it involved a media organization who then seemed to promote the fact that this was happening because it seemed to validate the importance of the organization.

EUGENE JARVIS, **Atari programmer:**

Gamergate was like some kind of attack on a girl or something?

CHUCK KLOSTERMAN, **author/pop-culture essayist:**

People kept saying, "This is not about sexism. This is about ethics in gaming journalism." I have *no idea* what they're referring to outside of the fact that there seemed to have been a situation where gaming journalists had a relationship with a game creator and there was an assumption that somehow this was promoting the game. To say that I followed it? I mean, I didn't follow it. I'm curious what was so important about it, to be honest.

LISA NAKAMURA, gender and technology researcher:
You know, what strikes me is that none of my students know what Gamergate is because it's been three years.* Well, now it's become a historical event. . . . You talk about it as an event that was important because it signaled the fall of the game industry at that period of time. One of the problematic things about Gamergate is that you couldn't say who won or lost. It just showed everybody's ass.

KUKHEE CHOO, media studies professor:
My understanding of Gamergate was that they actually, what? My understanding was there was a . . . I'm totally blanking on Gamergate. [Laughs] Just remind me?

ANDRÉS PERTIERRA, r/AskHistorians moderator:
Gamergate—I'm not really sure there is a really good parallel because of the very unique nature of the digital age, but it has some elements of a moral panic, which is something we're all familiar with. In the 1980s it was: Children are being molested at kindergarten. That was a huge bugbear for many years, even though there was no proof that this was happening disproportionately, and people were panicked about kids. Then, in the 1990s: Videogames are causing people to kill other people. There was that moral panic. There's tons of moral panics throughout history. I think [Gamergate] has that aspect to it because it has two sides to it—it was framed by supporters as a movement for "ethics in games journalism," which, that's not really what the movement was about.

The movement started as the "Five Guys burgers and fries" thing, which was a 4chan meme.† Then it got popularized on YouTube by

---

* Interview conducted October 10, 2018.
† In a November 2014 *Medium* article, "GamerGate and the New Misogyny," writer Jay Allen explains: "Gjoni accused Quinn of cheating on him with five different men, so Gjoni adds the little rhyme of 'Five guys?' and 'Burgers and Fries,' along with the logo of the Five Guys franchise hamburger chain. Gjoni encapsulated his anger with Quinn in a neatly portable meme, and all he needed was a pulpit and an audience."

YouTube reactionaries like Internet Aristocrat, who *is* a neo-Nazi and whose goodbye video was him literally quoting *Mein Kampf*, but that side of the moral panic was less focused. It was the "ethics," but it was more about a woman who sold herself. It's the cheating angle. That was the original hook.

The Eron Gjoni rather long blog post [from August 2014] about how his girlfriend cheated on him with a bunch of guys who . . . It's immaterial whether or not she did, because that was the original hook of the movement. If I recall correctly, the original blog post emphasized the "ethics" side less in terms of the games journalism. It was more about her having cheated on him. That was the original moral panic, and so it was about shaming her for having violated these social norms or having allegedly violated these social norms. That's where it started, and then it got co-opted into a much more explicitly political movement by these actors.

MAUREEN RYAN, *Variety* **TV critic:**
I was one of those people that fell down the rabbit hole of looking at Twitter threads and just trying to figure out . . . Gamergate took off not because it was a guy who was pissed about his girlfriend doing X or Y. It took off because it was a spark to a ginormous amount of tinder from an age ago. There's this incredibly diseased thought process at the heart of the Gamergate communities based on: "I've been hurt. Who has empathy for me?" And they would have it for each other. It's just all directed at those "who don't understand our culture, understand our world, cater to us, and validate us."

DIXON WU, Neo Geo World Tour organizer:
It's really hard to say 'cause . . . I think I remember this thing kind of happened, like four years ago?* At that time I was in Hong Kong, so naturally you won't expect the local news or media outlets would cover it. I've actually read this online. I've read this on North American websites or gaming websites. So, the perspective is naturally biased already, I would say. I don't think they have ever had people that are outside of this Gamergate thing really look into it and did any kind of reporting

---

* Interview conducted October 4, 2018.

on it. It was all within North America. That is why I think this thing was not really known to people in Asia, for example. So you would see all these online discussions about it and all these threats and all that. But us? I would say most of us didn't really even know that happened.

DAVID WEINBERGER, *The Cluetrain Manifesto* **coauthor:**
I hate talking about Gamergate. It should've been a learning moment in the way that #MeToo has been for many, many people and I'm sure was, but it escalated into doxing* and physical threats and people having to leave their homes to remain safe. So it certainly was a learning moment for many people, but it was very different than #MeToo, in which the culture seems to overall reject the idea that the victims of abuse should be further threatened. Gamergate turned in on itself and just escalated the ugliness beyond—*way* beyond—where it hadn't been. Gamergate was so intense and called up such ugliness in response to what should have been made a very clear learning moment that it's frightening. . . . The case I usually do not make, because other people are making it much better and I don't feel like I need to, but Gamergate is a really good example of the internet calling out the worst in people.

It was an opportunity to have your ears unplugged and your eyes open to what the experience of online gaming is for a very large segment of the population. But it wasn't. The reaction from the perpetrators was so vicious and over-the-top and escalating it beyond outside of the realm of just the digital out into the real world. That's unusual. It's not unprecedented, but it's unusual when it's so clear that there's injustice and unfairness and vulnerability and the reaction is, "Good, let's pile on and make it worse." That's unusual. Not unprecedented but unusual.

STEPHANIE HARVEY, *Counter-Strike* **world champion:**
I just remember people were confused about the situation. It was like a big bomb, but nobody really understood it well and nobody knew

---

* The act of maliciously researching and publicly sharing an individual's private information without consent, doxing is often used for online harassment. It can escalate to "swatting," involving false emergency reports that trigger an unwarranted and potentially dangerous response by law enforcement.

how to tackle it, and we just kind of ignored it. I just didn't want to be a part of it. So no one did anything 'cause the Gamergate trolls were bigger than the rest. Nobody touched it. I remember at that time I was working in game development and we did not even have an internal email. We didn't even get a, "Oh, this is happening, we are here for you." Nothing.

The amount of power they had, they had forums that were going on twenty-four hours and their only goal was to destroy that person's life from hacking personal information to where they were going next to how can we hurt that person the most in their career to digging everything they could on that person and try to make them lose money, employment, fear for their life. It went to the point in Gamergate that people actually tried to kill them in real life. I didn't want to be in that situation. It's as simple as that. I had the choice to kinda ignore it since I was a high-profile female at the time in gaming. I had the potential to be part of it and I did not have the energy to do that.

I didn't even want to answer an interview that could be linked to the word "Gamergate." If I was doing an interview and they would ask a question about Gamergate, I refused to have that question be posted, not even the tag #Gamergate, 'cause they have bots researching for Gamergate across the internet and as soon as they see it . . . I was even tagged in Twitter posts and I never replied, never did anything, and I would get *massive* amount of flood of people insulting me. And I had nothing to do with it. I just got tagged. As soon as you barely touched it, it became like *crazy*.

I don't think I can handle it as a human. I want to compete. And if I can't even go to tournaments, then it's gonna literally ruin my life. So I needed to take a step back and I did not speak up during Gamergate. I was not a part of it. I wanted to dodge the wave 'cause I knew I couldn't handle it. . . . I'm not scared of that wave anymore. But when it happened, even top celebrities that touched it almost got their life destroyed. If *they* were in that situation, then I couldn't imagine if that happened to me what would have happened.

CHRIS MANCIL, Electronic Arts global director of community:
Very broadly speaking, EA wanted this to be over. This isn't something we wanted to be a part of. We wanted to stay away. This was very

toxic and was hurtful for a lot of people. So from a corporate stand-point, threats are never acceptable anytime. But, I mean, conversations for people in the industry and stuff was like, this is really hard for folks because there were . . . It was terrible. There's games press who we've got relationships with and people that we know fighting with game celebrities on YouTube and Instagram and Twitter. Then there's people across all sides literally fighting about subject matter and topics that are important and should be debated, but the sad . . . The hard thing about Gamergate in a lot of ways was it was an amplification of culture wars and a medium that really hadn't had to deal with that very often.

SHANNON APPELCLINE, role-playing-game historian:

We very much have seen that type of thing in the tabletop role-playing* hobby as well. About 2012 was the first time I saw it as a flashpoint. There's been lots more discussion in that time period about diversity in the hobby, about women in the hobby, about harassment of women in the hobby. And a lot of it I think has been because a very small subset of people aren't happy about diversity or women in the hobby, that they feel vulnerable. They feel like they are losing their hobby.

CHRIS MANCIL, EA global director of community:

Gaming for the most part had been . . . where you escape to get away from some of that stuff, and then it became part of it. And then the worst tribal aspects of a lot of different people came together. And what was sad for me, because I made the mistake of getting involved with it and it was very hard and very damaging on me, was that there was no room—there was no goodwill and there was no ability to debate or have a conversation or just assume the best intentions from someone that you didn't agree with. And it was literally the worst elements of dehuman-ize and attack and destroy. It was the first signs of deplatforming and delisting and getting people fired that you don't agree with and doxing

---

* A form of interactive storytelling, often melded with strategic game elements, where players craft characters and journey through imaginary worlds, collaboratively shaping narratives via character actions, often with a game master's guidance. Think *Dungeons & Dragons*.

people. It was really just all-out warfare that was just very damaging. And to be honest, I think games was a backdrop. I don't fundamentally think it had a lot to do with games. Gaming was parts of it, but a lot of it had to do with people who just really wanted to fight about issues that were never really clearly identified completely for everyone. Or like they were arguing against different issues. It was just awful.

STEPHANIE HARVEY, *Counter-Strike* **world champion:**
It was as simple as any female that was touching the Gamergate issue, whether it's you tweet about it, whether you talk about it, there was not only robots looking for the word "Gamergate," [but] there was real people that would analyze where the word was said and all that. As soon as a woman in games would take a stand, whether it's a positive or negative or whatever, they had the potential to become a target to the Gamergate. Mainly, if you were targeted by Gamergate, I don't know exactly the amount of people that would start to harass you, but imagine one person throwing rocks versus a thousand people throwing rocks.

JASON DEMARCO, **Adult Swim senior vice president:**
It was a tempest in a teapot that went outside the teapot. Basically it was a bunch of people mad about *total bullshit* and then a bunch of other people creating lies to prop the bullshit up and then going out into the world and attacking everyone that they thought did these things or didn't do these things. And then it just turned into a giant scrum.

RICHARD BARTLE, **online game pioneer/researcher:**
I was surprised that Gamergate actually got any purchase, and that's probably what happened to the majority of the games industry. They were blindsided by it because they weren't expecting these people to be taken seriously. They're like flat-earthers: why would anybody treat them seriously? These people are the same. They're coming out with these outrageous opinions, behaving dreadfully in ways that really there should be laws against and there probably are.

MAUREEN RYAN, *Variety* **TV critic:**
If I look back at that time, I'm frankly disappointed in how few men just stood up and said, "What the fuck is wrong with you people? What

the fuck?" A lot of women were writing that. *A lot* of women. A lot of men dismissed it as not important. It kept getting worse. It never ended.

All of these Gamergate people are like, "Free speech! Free speech!" But as the saying goes, you can't shout fire in a crowded theater. It's like, I've been to Comic-Con. Not anything goes. If you just make a T-shirt online that has a DC character, you can't do that.

FLOURISH KLINK, *Fansplaining* cohost:
I don't think that I've used the word "Gamergate" on Twitter since it happened because I learned very quickly that if you use the word "Gamergate," then lo and behold, your life was nothing. [Laughs] You were just gonna get inundated with Pepes* and, fine, I don't have time for them.

HOWARD RHEINGOLD, virtual community pioneer/writer:
Gamergate was kind of the jumping-off point for what became the alt-right.

LINDA CARLSON, Sony Online Entertainment community manager:
Gamergate was a masterclass in the art of trolling and toxicity. The biggest problem is you'll never find two people who have exactly the same opinion of what Gamergate *even was*. It really just seemed to exist as a way for trolls to harass and bitch about everything, regardless of whether it was founded or not.

AMERICAN MCGEE, *Doom* designer:
The fact that nobody exactly knows what it is, is exactly the point of what it was. . . . Basically, we can all be looking at the same screen, but the audience is actually watching two different movies at the same time. If you were to try to stop audience A and bring their attention to the fact that movie B is playing, it won't work. They'll suffer massive

---

* Pepe the Frog originated in the online comic *Boy's Club* in 2005 and has subsequently taken on another life as an internet meme. Though innocuous at first, the character's evolution through repeated use by others gave rise to bigoted versions, especially on 4chan and Reddit. In response, the Anti-Defamation League collaborated with Pepe's creator, Matt Furie, in 2016 to reclaim the symbol from those with hateful intentions. Nevertheless, the stain remains on the character to this day.

cognitive dissonance and they'll run away because people perceive what they want to perceive.

I think the amazing ingenuity of Gamergate was that it was actually a giant nothing. But it was a giant nothing that no one can actually agree on what it was. There was never a resolution to it and it's still slung around like the word "Nazi" for gamers. If you don't come down on one side or the other of this, you're a bad guy.

CHUCK KLOSTERMAN, author/pop-culture essayist:

I think that if people have a cursory knowledge of what Gamergate is without knowing the specifics, they do know that fundamentally the idea is about sexism and the belief that the culture of gaming is misogynist, basically. Just that it's an inherent part of it. It has to do both with the majority of the people playing the games, the content of the games themselves. This spills into the idea of if this is a culture of people and it is dominated by men both in terms of participation and in terms of the content of what they're participating in—that this is a problem.

Whenever I saw people discussing Gamergate, it seemed as though their position on the specifics of the conflict were a political reflection of whether or not they agreed with the premise that games are sexist. If they believe that there is a degree of misogyny in playing videogames and in videogame culture, that's what Gamergate was really about. If they don't believe that, they think, "Well, this is people trying to find a reason to make that expectation."

DAVID WEINBERGER, *The Cluetrain Manifesto* coauthor:

I can't make sense of it, and I think it's because it is unusual, if not unique, in internet history in that it became about itself. It became so ensnarled and so fractal in its nature that the main question pretty quickly became what you make of Gamergate: Gamergate is about what you make of Gamergate. Do you think that this is about misogyny gone wild or do you think it's about, I don't know, lying, needy women who are responding to a bad breakup and just need to get laid?

There are other interpretations as well, but it became so self-referential and so much about what you thought Gamergate is about that actually the lines were drawn pretty quickly. Not between women and the men who were allies and the perpetrators but between what you think Gamergate is about. And those lines are pretty much gonna divide the world into pretty much the same sets of people. It's not unusual for the internet to go meta. Reddit is happily meta very, very frequently. A lot of Reddit humor is being meta about the thread and about the last comment. The net is making people more meta in their approach. It didn't begin with the internet. Ironic humor started doing this as well as other forms, but that was showing up in the culture before the internet.

The internet has let this escalate. And overall I think it's a really good thing. Overall, you can step back from even your own beliefs and look at them and make fun of them and maybe even start thinking about them differently. That's harder, but meta is a good evolutionary step for humans to take. Gamergate got that so looped that there was no way to escape it. That was another reason why it wasn't the learning moment that #MeToo was. #MeToo isn't about #MeToo. It's about the actual wrongs and the vulnerabilities. Gamergate lost sight of that really quickly. It was such a mess. That's why it was so hard to ever say anything about it in the midst of it. Probably now, as well.

It should have been 100 percent clear. It *really* should have been. . . . I don't think a lot of good came out of it and a lot of horrible things came out of it. But that should have been what we learned, just as from #MeToo we—by which, I mainly mean men—learned just how structurally misogynist most organizations are, even ones that don't intend to be. . . . Gamergate was not a useful experience overall. Is that mild enough? I mean, it was such a nightmare.

CHAPTER 2

JUST ANOTHER DAY
AT THE OFFICE

No Statements, No Accountability

LULU LAMER, videogame producer:

[Laughs] Well, as if the game industry is going to intervene, my ass. That's just a complete joke, imagining that the industry would do anything when there are so many of their own hiding in this. The idea that Gamergate was *just* toxic fans or people peripheral to the games industry is just absolutely not true. Basically every company had their own little Gamergaters hiding in the corners.

WAGNER JAMES AU, journalist/Second Life historian:

During Gamergate, I was saying more industry leaders should come forward. A really well-known designer was messaging me going, "You know, I get death threats all the time. I have a security guard." And I'm like, "Well, okay, yeah, that's a problem, but you probably don't have people threaten to rape you and kill your children. And in any case, why don't you say something about this?" [Their response was] something along the lines of, "It's not my responsibility."

There was a real omertà attitude: "Okay, we're not gonna talk about this." Or they would talk about it in back channels. But I think PR generally at companies said, "No, we are not talking about this at all." And they would also tell people at companies not to talk about it because it would end up several people got fired for talking about

Gamergate or talking about gamer privilege, complaining about it. They actually got fired.

STEPHANIE HARVEY, *Counter-Strike* world champion:
I remember during Gamergate, because I was one of the most vocal people at Ubisoft, a couple of us got trained for media for Gamergate and it was always like, "Don't answer these kinds of questions. Don't answer this. Just say this doesn't happen." And I remember I was sitting in the room and I looked at my HR and I said, "You realize that this is happening to me in the company right now with other employees, right? I'm not gonna say this doesn't happen."

It was something like, "My environment is safe, I never get harassed, or I never get discriminated because I'm a woman in my workplace." These kinds of things, or, "I don't feel that I am less respected because I'm a woman. I've never encountered something like that within my company." These kinds of things when *all* of those were lies. It was all males. I remember [the HR person's] face being like, "Well, can't you just say that?" And I remember the other women with me voicing up like, "Actually this happens to me too. I will not say that to the media. I will not say it doesn't happen when it happens." They were shocked: "What? This happens within the company?" And I'll be like, "Yeah, this happens on a daily basis with other coworkers. I'm not gonna go on the TV shows and say, 'Oh, but we're fine. In our company, everything is purple or pink.' No! This is straight-up a lie that I will not be a part of."

SERAPHINA BRENNAN, Warner Bros. Games community manager:
I've been on the receiving end of death threats, and other members of my company had security details attached to us as we walk[ed] to our cars because there were credible threats against us and our workplaces, which is scary. . . . When Gamergate happened and that really became the forefront, it was really only one very prominent company that said, "This is bad and we don't support it." Blizzard did it. They did it very prominently on their stage of BlizzCon,* and that was it.

---

* Annual gaming convention hosted by Blizzard Entertainment since 2005. BlizzCon serves as a platform for Blizzard to hype new games and provide an opportunity for its players to gather. The event, attracting fans from around the world, includes panels, a cosplay contest and exhibition, tournaments, and hands-on demos.

[Laughs] But a lot of other companies, and I hate to say this, but mine included, didn't want to deal with that. They didn't feel like that was their job. They looked at it and said, "Don't talk about it." In fact, when Gamergate was happening and I was in Warner Bros., they wanted to make sure that no one talked about it publicly.

People would drop by your desk or an email was sent out saying, "Hey, we know that there's Gamergate talk. Don't engage with it. And if you see it, just delete it." Like, if it's on our own forums—which, crapshoot if it is—you're not going to be able to control all of Facebook or all of Twitter or all of any of that. It was just: "Ignore it. It's not happening." At the same time, my information and one of my colleague's information—we sat next to each other—appeared on [far-right website] *Breitbart* because Milo Yiannopoulos felt it was appropriate to shove everyone's information online after finding out that some of us from the game-journalist scene were in a group together in the Yahoo! groups. I was one of those members.

Our information appeared on *Breitbart* as potentially some of these people who were pulling strings behind the scenes on review scores and collaborating like a shadow cabal, which wasn't the case. [Laughs] You know, completely not the case. We looked at each other and went, "Holy shit, we're being targeted. And our first response is do nothing?" [Laughs] Like, what do you mean *do nothing*? My information's out there and people think I'm this crazy shadow-cabal person. I'm not! I'm a person who sits here and wants to make better games and who loves games to death. It was frustrating to be sidelined effectively.

I had a Twitter war with Milo Yiannopoulos in DM because I was angry. I'm like, "Dude, you put my stuff online because why? You wanted clicks, effectively?" And of course at that point he called me a tranny fag because he does not like transgender people and I am transgender, and we just exchanged some heated insults and that was that. But I couldn't say anything about it online. I couldn't post what he sent to me because if I did, I could face punishment at my job.

ANGELINA BURNETT, *Halt and Catch Fire* **writer:**
There's two levels. There's the people who make the work in the industry and I think by and large they lean left. Then there's the economic decisions that have to get made by those who hold the purse strings and

they're not conservative or liberal. They are profit-driven, and I don't think that's good or bad. It just is. [Laughs] They look at the landscape and they make decisions based on what they fucking think will protect their shareholders. It's really cynical and simple, and sometimes that's a liberal decision and sometimes that's a conservative decision.

KATIE FLEMING, *Katie's Tomb Raider Site* **founder:**
Every studio has different policies and different ways of handling things. While the Gamergate thing was happening, studios should definitely have been more reactive legally. I would hope that if somebody was threatening me and showing up at my house that my studio would get their legal team involved and authorities, because if it becomes that personal you need to have that extra support. I don't know if those studios provided any or not. From things I'd seen about that behavior, there was no support. It was up to the individual to call the police if they felt threatened.

These people are all getting away with it too, right? There were no consequences. So if people are seeing there's no consequences, then they're more apt to do it. If the first time it happened when they showed up at somebody's house they were arrested and put in jail for five years, then maybe that would have had more of an impact. I forget the streamer—a few weeks ago,* during one of his live streams somebody drove by his house and was shooting his windows. If you see that nothing ends up happening, if they don't catch the person or put them in jail, then there's no consequence, so people will keep doing it. But especially if you're a public face of the game, the studio absolutely needs to support you.

STEVE SPOHN, The AbleGamers Charity COO:
It is obvious to me and doesn't even need to be spoken about that everyone should be against any human being being physically harmed, sexually assaulted, or mentally abused because of a decision they made in developing a videogame or promoting a videogame. It is not acceptable that I had to watch friends have their home addresses published on

---

* Interview conducted November 6, 2018.

Twitter and that there was nothing we could do to stop it. It was heart-breaking to see posts where people were talking about what kind of sexual things they were going to do when they got ahold of my friends.

As a whole, the industry needs to stand up to any entity that causes or seeks to cause harm against people in real life over the fictional world of videogames. When you have people who are pointing out the real-life information of where someone lives and how to get to them, then that is something that needs to stop. Now, there's no message from any company or any one person—no matter who they are—that can stop someone from doing that. Even if we remove it from Twitter or Insta-gram or Facebook, there are dark webs and there are channels where people are going to get this information. This is just a thing that's going to happen. No one person could have put a stop to it, but if enough of us stand up and just say, "That's not cool. That's not a way to fight your point of view," then maybe it'll be curbed and not quite so bad.

LINDA CARLSON, Sony Online Entertainment community manager:
The problem is the industry—two things. One, the industry didn't know what to do about it. Number two, when they were directly in-volved, they really tried to stay out of it as much as possible. Keep in mind I'm talking about managing them on channels that we actually control. For instance, if somebody starts writing hate speech on Twitter and I don't know who the player is, I can't do anything about it.

But if they start doing that either in our games or on our forums—if it's a place where I can actually have some say in how people behave—then I am able to do just like the pub owner: pick them up and set them out on the street. If you don't get satisfaction screaming at the CEO of a company, maybe you'll get satisfaction going to Reddit, which *nobody* controls. You start screaming there and people pile on, and I have cer-tainly seen staff from within the gaming industry [engage] who have perhaps been let go for reasons that I do not agree with. It seems to happen when the toxic crew gains a foothold on an external platform of communications that the game companies have no control over.

As a community manager, again, I liken it to running a pub. I'm not putting up with that behavior. Not in my house. And that comes straight down from the CEO, from the COO. We are not putting up with that in our pub. So if you want to do it, I'm sure you can find a dive bar a couple of blocks down the road where they allow you to open carry and do all sorts of other things. But I do agree that companies need to take a stand for what's right, at least within the confines of the milieu that we can control in-game, in our communication channels. Asking people to do anything beyond that is like asking Canada to go and arbitrate a civil war in Algeria or something like that. We just don't have the ability to do so.

That goes back to the old theory of "don't feed the trolls." That is certainly true to some extent when you've got a group that defies any rational discussion—the Gamergate group was one of those. . . . These people aren't really interested in making things better. They're interested in the attention it gets them, the fact that venting their spleen feels *good* to them. They're doing this for enjoyment and *that's* the problem. So there really is no point. The companies that I have worked for have steered clear of that sort of discussion because they know that there is no value to be had. . . . I'm going to go back to the fact that I don't think anybody really knew *what* to do.

ANDRÉS PERTIERRA, r/AskHistorians moderator:

If you're dealing with a harassment campaign being directed by people in bad faith, concessions won't work. They just won't. You're just setting yourself up to getting more harassment and theatrics.

SOREN JOHNSON, *Civilization IV* lead designer:

I remember there were a lot of attempts by groups to stand up for diversity: "Okay, we're a bunch of game developers, and we're gonna get together and make a statement about how we want to be inclusive, we want diversity in our games, in our audience." It didn't really make any difference. . . . I actually feel like we dealt with it as well as we could have.

KEN WONG, *Monument Valley* lead designer:

The games industry is not a monolith. Organizations like the International Game Developers Association, which is as close to being a representative of the entire industry, or the Entertainment Software Association, they did make statements against Gamergate. I was at the Independent Games Festival in 2015 and it was hosted by [game developer] Nathan Vella, and he made this very moving statement against Gamergate and he received like a five-minute standing ovation. It was incredible. It felt to me at the time that the industry was definitely against Gamergate. I don't know what a blanket statement from the industry would look like, really. People made petitions and people signed them, but it's not like there's one monolith.

SHANNON APPELCLINE, role-playing-game historian:

I would say a couple of strong statements is about the same thing as little to no intervention if there weren't any actual repercussions or results. It's very easy to say something and it's very hard to do something. If they made strong statements and then the games were just the same, that's pretty much the same as no statement at all.

ANGELINA BURNETT, *Halt and Catch Fire* writer:

What keeps occurring to me is: but who? "The gamer space" is not a fucking person. "The gamer space" can't do a fucking thing. So, who? There's no Steven Spielberg. There's no Joss Whedon. [Laughs] There's no one who is a holder of weight in that culture who could come out and say something. Maybe there is and I don't know about them, but who the fuck? *Who*? [Laughs]

JONATHAN COULTON, musician:

This is the problem: Gamergate was a distributed attack. It's unclear who even was responsible for responding. So, I don't know what the answer is. I'm trying to think of an entity that I would have expected to do something differently. Aside from, I don't know: EA releases a statement about what? [Laughs]

JOI ITO, MIT Media Lab director:

It reminds me a little bit of Mark Zuckerberg. I don't think the people who run these game companies . . . I mean, they get those questions now when they're on panels, but it just hasn't been in their mindset that it's their job. Worrying about diversity. Worrying about: What do our players do when they're on social media? But this idea that they're socially responsible for things like Gamergate, I think the people in the big companies have never been like that.

But it's similar with Facebook. I think they denied it and denied it, and I think they had denied it in earnest, right? I think they thought, "No, we're neutral platforms. We're just algorithms. I don't want to be an editor and we're not." And it wasn't until you basically drag them in front of Congress before, "Oh, wait a second." I don't think that's happened to the game companies.

Getting dragged in front of Congress is a rite of passage. Yahoo! got dragged in front of Congress [by the World Organization for Human Rights USA in 2007] for giving email information of a Chinese dissident for privacy and human rights–related stuff. And so the more recent thing is the social media stuff, but I don't think game companies ever had that moment where it's more than this drone.

TIM LONGO, *Halo* creative director:

There's responsibility to protect employees and shed light on the conversation. I'm just making up numbers, but in that analogy of it takes a village to raise a child: If there's five pillars of the community and three of those choose not to engage, then the other two groups are now taking on all of the burden of raising this child. [During Gamergate] I don't think all the pillars stood up there, no. I don't even know if I could speak to what those are, which each pillar exactly was. That's not even me trying to avoid it. I just don't even know if I'm qualified or educated enough myself to say. I felt like at least when you see the articles and the stories and the videos that were out there, it feels like the victims were the ones that were bearing most of the burden.

I think in general people should know that game developers are people too, and we do hear this stuff. Not everyone carries that same culture that people are complaining about. [There are studios] trying to fix it both in the content itself and in policy and in studio culture. No studio culture is perfect, for sure, but there's always a conversation about it.

WAGNER JAMES AU, journalist/Second Life historian:

There's this fear that an experience with a rabid fan base getting out of control. They're afraid there's suddenly going to be a boycott protest against them on Reddit if they come out and say something too stridently. The industry is of gamers, by gamers. So it's a lot of people in the industry going, "Oh, come on. I get death threats all the time. What's the big deal?" Literally. I wish I could name names, but it's household names or as close to household names as you can get saying, "Look, I get death threats. What's the big deal?" So there's that. There was very generic statements. I remember at GDC* there was some sort of generic thing about, "Well, we're for all gamers, etc."

There's what the industry can do in a leadership role and there's what companies can do, even if we're not seeing enough on the leadership side in public. . . . The female user base for games is getting larger and larger every year. So they're stupid if they just let this stuff slide.

MAUREEN RYAN, *Variety* **TV critic:**

I just wanted some executive to stand up and say, "I have political capital, social capital within my firm and within my community. I choose not to use it on misogyny, bias, and racially exclusive hiring in my community. I choose not to spend my influence dollars in those directions." Okay, well, at least you said it.

Man, Hollywood's fear-driven, but I think the gaming industry is worse. It's all fear-driven: "Will people buy this? Will people buy it again? Do they want the same thing as before or close to the same thing as before?" Just not rocking the boat. It's funny because I think that they saw themselves as rebels and as these cool guys, but it's very conformist and it's very risk-averse in its current incarnation.

People don't want to be seen as making a decision. The thing is they have made decisions at every step of the way. They don't want to be called on it, though. They are very invested, especially the videogames companies. There's a sunk-cost situation where it's like, "Well, we've come this far and we haven't made real change." That's actually what's at the heart of all of this. You have to stand for something. Do they really all wanna go to their graves thinking, "Well, I got those games out on time!"

---

* The Game Developers Conference, held annually in San Francisco, is a gathering for professionals in the game industry. GDC encompasses lectures, panels, and networking opportunities. Beyond the formal sessions, at GDC there are also lots of informal and primarily social get-togethers—lots of parties, lots of drinking.

RON MEINERS, *The Sims 3* community manager:

I raised this presentation [three years ago*] of how one might have conflict-oriented games, and I suggested a nominal fee for creating an honorable play space. So you have basically two tiers of competitive games, and one of them, it's the usual crap, whatever goes on, and in the other one you need to maintain a positive reputation or get booted out. This is a space that is explicitly nontoxic, and it calls for a registration and it calls for a verifiable identity. It costs you a dollar a year, but it creates a space where the majority of people are going to have much more satisfying results. This was a very high-level management person, and the answer I was given was, "We can't take that potential loss of profitability by excluding gamers who wouldn't comply." That it was absolutely a question of, "We're gonna scrape the bottom of the barrel for every penny." That's what I was told. And again, this is somebody I have great respect for who I'm not gonna name, and I absolutely believe he was being straight with me.

Gaming spaces are too internally focused. They're too much concerned with the minutiae of their own competitions. Whereas Facebook or Google or Twitter—I don't know if there's any more altruism there, but gaming is just too competitive for its own good. People want success there too much, and it tends to be a detriment in terms of really great long-term thinking about how to proceed effectively. But a place like Facebook? Facebook *has* to solve this problem. They go down if they don't figure out how to make it a more reliable space, more protected space. Once it becomes clear that we need to start figuring this out and then people are doing it, then it'll migrate to games.

LINDA CARLSON, Sony Online Entertainment community manager:

I think we're all starting to look to these social sites to see: "Okay, so you guys have all the money, you have all the staff you could possibly want. What are you doing about it?" Because I think that we have a lot to learn from them if they could find a way to make people behave more decently toward one another. But again, it's the human species. I don't know if that's necessarily possible at this time.

---

* Interview conducted November 19, 2018.

DAVID WEINBERGER, *The Cluetrain Manifesto* **coauthor:**

So the game industry is saying that the solution to online game tox-icity has to come from Facebook? How does that even happen? What do they have in mind for that? Seriously. I don't understand that at all. I don't know if they have something in mind that is gonna work, but it seems unlikely as long as two bros or whatever can be racist—and homophobic and sexist doesn't even begin to cover it—and [they] feel good about it because they're congratulating, they're high-fiving each other, so to speak, then the game company has a problem that Face-book isn't gonna solve.

CHRIS MANCIL, EA global director of community:

I got drawn into it because I'm someone who deals with gamer communities, and as someone who's a community manager, I think of communities as my children. I'm very protective of them. Even the bad ones. I love gamers and I love gaming communities. My role has always been shepherd and manager of gamer communities, and I felt like there was a lot of attacks and misinformation from people attacking gamers as a class and gamer culture as a class. I didn't agree with it because there are bad elements in gaming, but I felt like there was a really broad brush that painted millions and millions of people as these awful, terrible people who hated women and hated liberal institutions and democracy and lots of other things. It struck me the wrong way because it wasn't my experience.

I started seeing things on Twitter that really concerned me where lots of media types and even gamers were creating these bots that would basically say, "You're either with us or against us." I had an incident on my Twitter where I lost five thousand or ten thousand Twitter followers overnight because I retweeted someone who was very disliked and probably deservedly so disliked. If you associate with certain people that are persona non grata, you will be automatically added to these ban lists, and so I was added to these ban lists. I wrote a blog post about it. I was concerned about this development, about where we would get to a place that we would have broad-based guilt by association software that would segregate us based on our friends list or based on our profiles but not necessarily based on our actions. That was concerning for me because I think that that would be the antithesis of what is promising about the internet as a place to bring people together and share experiences.

That was my time back then. I was a little naïve, because the reality is that there were really bad people on both sides of the argument. And there are folks like me who tried to get involved for good reasons but quickly became pawns or wind up going down a path that pretty much assured one side or the other would destroy us. It was awful. What I've come to see now, reflecting on it as that has passed, the reality is that there isn't a lot of great safeguards and tools for really bad people online. There isn't a good way to protect yourself if you have an unpopular opinion and suddenly a million people decide to tell you how awful you are as a person.

Our social media platforms today can put a tremendous amount of pressure or scrutiny on an individual that's *really* tough to bear. People can lose their jobs. People could say the wrong things. The promise of online digital communities where you could have these online societies and have debates and conversations and friendships got to a place where if you say the wrong word at the wrong time or like the wrong person or say the wrong joke, you could be destroyed and basically tarred forever. And I don't think Gamergate was necessarily the first part of that but was a sign of change online where there are certain things that are just off-limits. When you have large, really strong fights between large groups of people like that, the wise move is to stay out of it as much as you can because there's no winning there.

It's a tough one, man. It's a really tough one. Maybe there's peaks and valleys of how societies and cultures evolve and change, but we're not in a period right now where there's a great deal of debate and trying to get consensus and understanding and respecting your opponents. Certainly in America we're very divided and divisive. From a business perspective, the number-one thing is none of us have the moral authority to jump into a two-person argument and try to referee and manage that. I think what the games industry did was the right thing, which was express our fundamental value that gaming is for everyone.

GINA HARA, filmmaker:
I honestly think it comes down to technicalities and legal obligations that prevent these companies from putting out an apology. I think it's

not right. There should be apologies made. [Sighs] I don't know if that's even possible. They could definitely try better. At the end of the day the most important thing is doing better currently and the next time.

But yeah, it's shitty when you mess up and you don't apologize. I think what often happens with people, too, is that they mess up and in that moment we don't believe it's our fault, and then a year later, three years later, they look back and we realized we were total idiots. [Laughs] And then it's really awkward to put out an apology later. So I guess all you can do is do better.

MAUREEN RYAN, *Variety* **TV critic** :

The game companies are where Hollywood was twenty years ago. They have no clue. They stick their head in the sand. They wanna just think it's just going to blow over and it's a bunch of whiners: "Why do people keep complaining about this shit?"

SERAPHINA BRENNAN, WB Games community manager:

We didn't show a united front. . . . If all the gaming companies stepped up at the same time, makers of things that people love, it would've had more of an impact. We would have bolstered each other, but that didn't happen. Most gaming companies stayed silent and let it happen and hoped it would blow over. But I don't think it ever did. I think it changed everything from that point forward about what you could expect from an interaction and how defensive we got. We were so concerned at any point we could be facing another Gamergate or we could be facing another backlash about what we do and the things we do, especially with women. Anyone who was different.

For companies I worked at and the things I saw, there was never an issue of they wanted to stand up against misogyny, because at that point there was so much toxicity that it was just another page in the book. Like, "Oh, you got another harassment and death threat? K. We're gonna get those every day. Don't respond to it and make it worse, and don't make it worse because that can lose us money." It's not that they didn't want to stand up against the misogyny. It's that it was seen as just another day.

.

CHAPTER 3

IT CAN'T BE THAT BAD

The Women's Work of Untangling Workplace Misogyny

NOLAN BUSHNELL, Atari cofounder:
Every time I see an article claiming sexism in the game business, I give it really short shrift. . . . I tend to be very skeptical.

BRENDA LAUREL, Purple Moon cofounder:
[Nolan Bushnell] will never change. He will never change. He will never see it. His memory is of that randy-ass time when he had people in the hot tub and everybody seemed to be enjoying themselves. So that's invisible to him. He's never going to be able to see that because of the context in which he behaved in the past. It's unfortunate, but it's true.

EUGENE JARVIS, Atari programmer:
I think it was a shock to see just how oppressive it was to women in the environment. For many years there were very few women in the industry at all. It was like the guys in the auto-repair place with their Snap-on tools, babes on the wall. [Laughs] It was like this male locker room and we finally realized—I guess there was a moment of growing up: "Hey, probably more than half the gamers are women and this is the trash that's going around."

It's a growing-up thing of the industry that it's no longer a locker room. It was shocking to see where it was. I think because it was such a male-dominated industry for many years, we didn't realize how hostile the environment really was. We always said, "Well, women aren't really interested in games." But I think a lot of it was the environment. It certainly didn't help the recruiting process.

BRENDA LAUREL, Purple Moon cofounder:

I can remember going to my first hackers conference in 1986 and I was holding a little session for the eleven women there. [Laughs] It was on feminism and stuff like that and some men from Lucasfilm came because I was producing, at that time, for Activision. I think they were just there out of kindness because they were buddies. But I can remember just asking the question: "Why aren't there more women in this community?" And one of the men from Lucasfilm, who was an old-school nerd—we're talking poor personal hygiene, overweight, junk food–eating dude—said, "Did it ever occur to you that we don't want to work with you? We don't want to be around you?"

That was a real wake-up call to me. It had never occurred to me. I just felt the field was infected because of its origins and because we had no breakthrough products where women were major audiences.

I said, "No, it never occurred to me. Thank you for sharing." It was important that he said that. It must have cost him something. And it got us right down to the truth, at least the truth for that guy, and gave us a much more robust conversation almost immediately because people weren't pussyfooting. So I've seen the ethos of the male game developer change radically from those days of those nerds to people who are much more, you know, balanced. . . . But generally speaking, I have a network of friends who are game devs and acquaintances and we communicate about the workplace and I hear nothing but horror stories from women. It is a drag.

CLARINDA MERRIPEN, videogame operations director:

One of the first companies I worked with had one male and several female programmers from our Korean publisher. The male had taken their passports, would not let them talk to anybody. They had to live in the same apartment. It was weird. They weren't on the right visas. The whole thing was illegal all the way around. Within a week of me getting there, I say, "Look, this smacks of not only are we using them for their programming skills, but it's verging on what I think could be sexual slavery." And the CEO said, "Well, it's not our problem. We didn't hire them." And I'm like, "Don't you care?" I didn't say that, but I'm screaming in my head, and I had to get them moved out because the whole situation was nuts.

LULU LAMER, videogame producer:

The day before I started working at Ion Storm [in 2000]—I was the first woman ever hired there—[studio director] Warren Spector went around to everyone at the office and made them take down the porn off their walls because I was starting. Warren told me himself.

That implies he didn't have the moral fortitude to ask for it on his own behalf, though he told me he was offended by it and didn't like the culture it represented. The fact that he invoked me to do it meant that he also in some way "blamed" me, though I didn't ask for it, and I was placed in the position of being the moralizing, civilizing nanny voice before I even arrived. He didn't encourage it—that kind of culture isn't his thing in the slightest—but I don't think he knew how to stop it. It would require engaging with and talking about some sticky feelings and ideas. In Warren's case, I had the impression the whole thing was too base to talk about. Games studios get culturally stuck in so many ways on the hard conversations. Cultures solidify as the people who were initially unable to resolve the problem leave, but the processes to work around them remain.

Apparently in 2000 that was fine, but after that it wasn't. It was: Well, once there was a single woman, it was not fine anymore. I think that that baseline expectation—which obviously should have been the baseline expectation before I showed up—is pretty clear now.

EUGENE JARVIS, Atari programmer:

I don't think we had that degree of sophistication. You're just trying to make a buck and sell the next game. [Laughs]

AL LOWE, *Leisure Suit Larry* creator:

We were never criticized for being inclusive or not. I don't remember that ever coming up. Our big problem was to get out the next game.

Our big problem was get to work. We gotta get a game shipped by November. Everybody's focus was really on creating product and improving on what we'd done before.

MAUREEN RYAN, *Variety* **TV critic:**

Some of the first stories I did on representation and inclusion, I think I fell victim to that too: "But things are probably getting better?" I don't know why I said that. [But later, I got backlash] *all the time*. "I know four women who are working, so it can't be that bad." Or taking anecdotal data that you've seen in your day-to-day life and applying that to the whole industry. It's like—I'm really glad you work with four women out of the sixty people on your staff. That's not nothing. "Well, no one is sexist against them." I'm like, "Really? You follow them around 24/7?" That's weird and creepy. Don't do that. Way before #MeToo, I would say it's *Mad Men*, but worse. People would be like, "Wait, now?" Like, "Yeah, now." Then [#MeToo] came along and I was like, "I told you."

Even today I have executives at TV studios or networks telling me, "All the women around me are telling me everything is great." I'm like, "Really? You wouldn't happen to have an absolute shit-ton of power over their careers, would you? What else are they gonna tell you?" [Laughs] Were you born yesterday? What's wrong with you?

LULU LAMER, **videogame producer:**

There've been too many harassment suits at smaller companies, at tech companies in male-dominated industries, that you just can't do overt stuff anymore. Someone told me recently that they were shown by a coworker an explicit image really very soon after starting and after complaining to HR, because it was apropos of nothing, they were told, "Well, this is an artistic industry and the person was just sharing an appreciation for art with you."

CLARINDA MERRIPEN, **videogame operations director:**

Most developer HRs came up from being office managers and had no idea what they were doing and how to grow and figure out the role, which is the same as any small business. As more money started coming in, they started realizing this was more important. In HR, you get three kinds of people: you get social workers, which are terrible; you get people who are yes-men for the company and those are also terrible; and then you get people who are really smart. If you're really smart, you don't always go into HR. I'm serious. If you've got that kind of brain, you tend to go into other things. But the best companies have really active, creative people in HR.

But you still grapple with things like, "Oh look, the nude picture of the anime girl, is that offensive or not offensive? Am I raising waves by saying you have to take that down? Are they gonna make fun of me? Are they going to listen to me?" These are the same conversations you have in all these other corporate cultures, because boys will be boys, except now we know that you don't have to let boys be boys.

I can tell you a story. When I was speaking at the Game Developers Conference, GDC, I was asked to a lunch with Microsoft and I spoke after the VP of something and he was saying, "If you're good, keep your head down, do your work and do that, do this, do the other thing." And I basically came up behind him and said, "Forget all he said. He's wrong. You have to shine. You have to be the best you can be. Don't put your head down. Don't shut up. Don't let anybody walk all over you. I agree, you have to be great, but why do we have to be quiet about it? Why do we have to be not shiny?" I got a standing ovation, though I'm sure the VP was looking at me funny. I was much more polite about it, but I was very loud. I'm like, "No, well-behaved women rarely make history." The [historian Laurel Thatcher Ulrich] quote, something I lived by. If you are well-behaved, if you shut up, if you take it, that's where you're gonna live your life, and it's going to mean that you'll never be heard.

The whole idea that you don't say anything when someone makes a bad joke: Why do you want to live in that kind of environment? And by a bad joke, I mean super-sexist, racist, transphobic, homophobic, all that stuff. [Sighs] Why do I want to work at a place where they wrap a cord around Barbie's breasts 'cause they're trying to focus on breasts for a breast-physics engine? No. Uh-uh. I'm sure there's better ways you can do that. You don't have to do *that*. [Laughs] That is a terrible thing. And it's completely unhelpful and you can't tell me that any of that makes any sense in anybody's head.

LULU LAMER, videogame producer:

I remember talking to my mom about work for the first time when I was managing a bunch of quality-assurance folks at Looking Glass Studios [in 1998]. There was a guy in the group who was really, really smelly and nobody wanted to sit by him, but we had to because we're all in this area of cubes. I was like, "Oh God, this is the worst. I don't know how to talk about things to people." And my mom was like, "Look, I've had this plenty of times. Sit him down and say, 'Listen, you have to take a shower every day and use soap and use deodorant afterwards.'" I was like, "Oh my God, you say all that stuff?" She was like, "Yeah, you have to. Yeah, you gotta go all the way down in level of detail. If you have to tell somebody they have to shower, you probably also have to explicitly tell them to wear clean clothes the next day."

It was really not specifically vocally sexist and shitty, but it was still not tremendously comfortable for a young woman. I was very young when I started. I was twenty-two. So while we're working late on *System Shock 2*, I had a tiny, tiny little office across from the rest of quality assurance and all of these people would creep around my door to hang out and chat and all kind of showing off a little, trying to be a little bit clever, interesting, make me laugh and stuff. It was years later that I was like, "Man, that was creepy." [Laughs] That there was a component in that attention that was specifically about my gender.

NOLAN BUSHNELL, Atari cofounder:

One of the big problems that we had is there are just not enough good female employees for the game business. . . . If I said that I demand we get a female game programmer, I don't think that we could accomplish that in a year if we were willing to pay double what a normal programmer was. I mean, they're just not there. They could be making triple what they're currently making. It's just bizarre to me. [Laughs]

KEN WONG, *Monument Valley* lead designer:

Wasn't *Centipede* programmed by a woman? There have been female game developers from the very beginning, but I think as games got more sophisticated and games wanted to be taken seriously—one way to do that is to tell adult stories, which became about sex and violence. So it was one thing leading to another, which just generated this idea that games are for men and by men. Then that majority wants to protect itself and then you have these people saying, "Well, we should just hire the best person no matter what gender they are," not taking into account that women have to work harder for that and women get paid less.

They're just not acknowledging that there are invisible biases and they're not willing to take a look at themselves and question: Are there things that I'm doing but I'm not even aware of? I think for a lot of men, because they haven't done the reading, the way men see themselves is: I don't rape women and I don't harass women, therefore I'm an okay guy. They look at society and they're like, "Women like wearing makeup and they like wearing high heels and they like feeling sexy. Cosplayers like wearing sexy clothes. Why can't I design characters that are sexy and like to show off their bodies?"

HEATHER CHAPLIN, author/media critic:

I gave a talk at GDC in 2007, 2008, where I was trying to address the question—everybody was really concerned at that time about why games didn't get the respect that they felt that they deserved. I used to spend a lot of time talking about that issue in mainstream channels and defending the industry and explaining why it was valuable and valid and not this terrible thing. In this talk, I said I was sick of playing that role and that if game developers wanted their industry to have the respect of other "art forms," then they had to grow up and stop acting like a bunch of disgusting teenage boys and produce material other than just adolescent male power fantasies and women in bikinis and shooting shit up. I had this whole riff about, like, grow up and be a man. Don't just stop at being a guy, don't just be an adolescent boy. Be a man. Not in the gender sense, but in the sense of *stand* for something. Push something. Be brave. Don't just produce this crap.

The reaction was really intense. I had some supporters. [Game developer] Clint Hocking or somebody told me he almost got in a fistfight over it in the hallway of GDC. [Laughs] Because he thought it was a good talk. It *really* riled people up. They made me cry, which I don't do very often. I got so much nasty—like, people on their blog. It wasn't social media yet, but the internet was there, and designers who I thought were my friends being like, "Who is this bitch and is she on her period? How dare she!" It was nuts.

MAUREEN RYAN, *Variety* TV critic:

I've been writing about issues to do with culture for twenty-six, twenty-seven years. And this really applies to way beyond any culture industry: What are you willing to do to protect members of your community from a sociopath or clinical narcissist who regularly inflicts pain and is smart enough to evade capture and notice? What are you going to do? What are you willing to do? There are people who are willing to inflict harm who are smart, who are savvy, who are clever, who are willing to lie, willing to gaslight people, willing to lie to themselves. They tell a story to the world about who they are, but their actions tell a different story. And once you're aware of those people, what are you going to do? I can't think of another community in which those types of people are not only enabled and ignored but actually kind of valorized in some ways. The videogame world is the worst for that. Quite frankly, it's got way too much of a soft spot for that sort of person.

HEATHER CHAPLIN, author/media critic:

I remember going to an Xbox party [at GDC in 2002] and I was hanging out with—I won't say who—a *very* successful game designer because I was writing about him for a magazine. He was introducing me to people as a prostitute working the party and he didn't seem to think that was inappropriate. He didn't even seem to know that that might not be wise in front of a journalist who's going to be writing about him.*

I remember at one point as the party progressed, I was standing on the staircase—thumping techno music—and just looking around and being like, "I'm the only woman I can see and this is dangerous." People

---

* Via email, Heather later confirmed as of 2019 that this person still works in video-games, writing: "He still is in the industry. And I don't remember anyone's reactions [at that party] in particular. I certainly don't remember anyone being shocked or telling him to stop." In 2024, Heather also emailed, "I believe he is at least videogame adjacent" and working in tech.

have been drinking. I remember a palpable sense of fear coming over me for my actual safety. When Gamergate broke, I didn't really follow it in terms of how the industry handled it. I just remember thinking about those incidents.

NOLAN BUSHNELL, Atari cofounder:

I was very progressive. I had equal pay, equal work. I hired women for senior positions, promoted from within. What was really powerful for Atari was we tried to be a perfect meritocracy, and when you're a perfect meritocracy there is no way for the normal discriminations of gender or sex or race to come in. You just want the best person, period. Very simple.

MAUREEN RYAN, *Variety* TV critic:

I remember a showrunner I actually really respect sitting on a panel in 2005 saying, "Hollywood's a meritocracy. The person with the best script wins." And I was like, "No, that's not true. That's not true at all." I would love it if 5 percent of the people that make decisions in the world of gaming were aware that they didn't live in a meritocracy. I think 5 percent would be generous.

Everyone who's involved in their storytelling endeavor thinks that they're on a hero's journey and they're a hero. If you were on a hero's quest, which is what so many videogames are about, you don't wanna hear that it's harder for somebody else. Yes, of course, you did face obstacles. You did have problems. You did almost not make it. You did have to work very hard. Undoubtedly. But you have blinders on to the people who were right beside you and dropped away. And if you did see them drop away, you attributed that to a decision that they made.

One thing I say a lot is the best and the worst thing about Hollywood is that it's made up of storytellers. I would imagine the same holds true for videogames. Because you want to believe an ending that feels cathartic, that feels conclusive and emotionally valid. It's satisfying. So you always put the ending on the story that isn't actually there.

You're not there. Your industry is not there. Your industry is a hotbed of misogyny and you're choosing to ignore it. If everyone was given the same opportunities and access and had the same formal and informal professional networks, 42 percent of your staff would be women and 40 percent of your staff would be people of color. If it's not, then it's you that's fucking up. It's your company that's fucking up. It's not those people.

Again, it comes into the sunk-cost thing. For someone who is an introverted gaming nerd who only just wants to code or make games or do something technical, they don't want to and think they shouldn't have to think about this other stuff that's irrelevant to them. It could have been relevant to them, but they chose not to make it that because their community told them this is bullshit and you don't have to listen to it. It's like, well, you really should have listened to it.

It can be painful to come down from a position that you decide is no longer morally defensible and that would require publicly admitting mistakes were made. It's not something that they are interested in.

CLARINDA MERRIPEN, videogame operations director:
One of the things that always struck me as insane is you have a chance to make X amount of money by behaving professionally. You choose not to do so because of some entitlement sense of who you have been, who you are, who you see yourself as being. That is the dichotomy that especially as a consultant I always had to navigate. Ostensibly they hire me to make them money, but in the end it's all about dealing with the personalities. That always confused me. I mean, it doesn't confuse me. I understand human nature. But it was always one of the center things that I always had to go back and forth between. The times that it didn't make sense really made me insane.

And that's all reflected in the games that they create and the decisions they make, because everybody's involved at different levels of the companies. So when you see this or you're part of this, you don't question the decision on how hard a female versus male character will hit in a game or what kind of clothes the character will wear. But the guys who are doing these kinds of things are reflected in the things that they do. I mean, none of this stuff is separate from that.

BEVERLY KEEL, Change the Conversation cofounder:
Sometimes I say to myself, "How didn't he or she know that they couldn't say that?" Meaning even if they felt that way, how didn't they know expressing that probably would get them in trouble? Whether

it's Roseanne Barr, whether it's someone making a racist or sexist statement or a joke about rape. Even if you feel that way personally, how are you so unaware of society that you don't know you can't say that without repercussions?

I think with sexual harassment, the message is out: You can't do it anymore. It's illegal and you will be punished. So even if you wanna do it, even if you personally think it's okay, now you have to worry about losing your job and getting sued or prosecuted. And then hopefully guys might say to their friends, "Dude, that's not cool. You could get in trouble doing that." So there will even be informal policing in their workplace.

I think we're in a transition time. Has it stopped? No. I would say just a slim majority of sexual-harassment victims have spoken up, but we're getting there.

BRENDA LAUREL, Purple Moon cofounder:

It's really, really complicated. It's not just that men behave badly. It's that we let them. We behave badly sometimes, too, when we don't know any better. It takes time to learn that blowing off steam and yelling at people, although men get away with it, is probably not a good idea, that there's a better way to communicate that makes the whole community more civil. That's hard to do when you're being a male impersonator trying to work your way through an organization.

BRIAN MCCULLOUGH, internet historian:

This is a thing that has shifted in culture. It was expected. If you haven't seen it, there's a documentary of Netscape from [2000, *Code Rush*] and it's behind the scenes and you see the engineering culture. It's all men. It's all super-bro-y. There's a couple women there, but they sort of hang around in the background.

If you read Anthony Bourdain's [2000] book, his first one, *Kitchen Confidential*, it hasn't aged well because when he talks about it, he's like, "Well, if you're gonna work in a kitchen and you're a woman, you've gotta be a tough broad that can roll with the punches and you gotta give as good as you can get and you gotta accept harassment, almost. If someone pats you on the butt, you kick him in the balls." That sort of thing. Before he died [in 2017] I saw him give interviews where he said, "Yeah, I regret that. I can't imagine how many people didn't go into my line of work because why should that be accepted?"

So I'm mentioning that Netscape documentary because what I took away from it was: "Well, listen, we're boys that are gonna be boys, and we're gonna fart and we're gonna curse and we're gonna make gay slurs and things like that, because if you want to work in this culture, this is how it is." And that's the thing that has changed even in the last ten years where it's like, "No, fuck that. Just because this is the industry and it's mostly male doesn't mean we have to accept that."

Were there things where people were harassed and there was a big scandal? No, because if you were a woman that went to work at Netscape in 1997, you expected to be treated badly. I'm not saying that like . . . I'm saying that like that's a shame. That's a tragedy. And hopefully that's what's changed, but there weren't any of those scandals unless something *really* horrible happened because it was accepted. This is a male-dominated, aggressive culture. And like Anthony Bourdain said in the book, if you want to work in the kitchen, it was expected that you had to be one of them brassy broads that wouldn't take any shit and the men came to respect you for it. And now society has moved on and evolved and we're like, well, it doesn't have to be that way.

BRENDA LAUREL, Purple Moon cofounder:

I think there were a lot of individual sadnesses as, one by one, we discovered, "Uh-oh, we're in trouble here. There's a serious dysfunction around women." And this probably happens to women in any workplace where you go in all bright-eyed and bushy-tailed and you think you've got stuff to offer and then reality seeps in and you realize, "Oh, I see. They're not listening to me. They're pushing me around. They're grabbing my ass. They're cutting lines of cocaine on their desk and asking me to snort them."

I started in the game industry in '76. I started at Atari in late '79 and I was at Atari from '79 to '83. I was an ass bandit. I hit on men. I had relationships with coworkers, and it didn't get clear to me until about three years in—because I was just ignorant, autistic me—that there was an imbalance going on, and that men were pushing me around and that it wasn't actually okay for a guy to throw me up against the wall in a hotel during the Consumer Electronics Show and try to tongue-kiss me. I came of age, in a way, at that company, and I went in with this lighthearted hippie abandon. These were pretty raucous days.

A lot of us came in as innocents and didn't realize that in a way we were giving everybody permission to do what they're doing today because in the beginning you behave differently. You don't know what's coming. You don't know if you're twenty-five and playful how you're contributing to the problem yourself. And I had to find that out. It took me some time to find out that *my* behavior was not great in terms of discouraging bad stuff. Then you get into phase two where you become a male impersonator because that's the way you get power. And I went through that phase two, and it kind of worked, but it sure wasn't fun and it wasn't comfortable and I wasn't able to contribute what I might have because I was being somebody I wasn't.

The sadnesses come and then you construct some other way to be. And the male-impersonation thing probably doesn't happen as much now. I'd be surprised if it did, because that's a response from some-body who's really isolated and alone, and there are enough women in the industry now that it may be that that's not as easy or an obvious choice. But these women just drag themselves around in sadness and shame and anger today and feel that they're trapped and that they have no way out and that nobody else is going to hire them because they'll get blackballed by the boys club. Sadly, that is true. So they feel stuck.

CLARINDA MERRIPEN, videogame operations director:
I think if you talk about powerlessness, you're doing a huge disser-vice to all the women who have spoken out and have had their lives disrupted around this and who have shown how brave they are. Young women—and I see this through my kids—have a different level of tol-erance and their tolerance is much lower for this kind of bullshit. As where when I was growing up, I was still coming off the '70s and '80s, which is you just stomach it and go on. There's less tolerance for that now, and rightly so. You don't put up with someone wrapping cords around Barbie dolls hanging at work. It's not a thing that you wanna walk by and see. It's not a thing that anybody should have to.

I also think that quite frankly, like me, if you work in this and somebody shoves your nose in shit for X period of time, after a while you're like, "I don't want my nose shoved in shit. I'm a valuable person.

I know what I'm worth outside of here. I can go someplace else and make *more* money and not have to deal with you." [Laughs] I mean, honestly, you don't have to be subject to this stuff and if you're smart and you're subject to this stuff, over a period of time you realize: I can be as famous or make as much money or be as happy someplace else, still have a connection to videogames in my independent time, or have people like me pay me stupid amounts of money to give them advice but not have to be there every day and deal with the shenanigans that go on.

LULU LAMER, videogame producer:

I really don't know. I feel like the industry as a whole has gotten a lot more professional, which is nice to see. I think there's a baseline expectation of people's behavior in their speech at work that is respected, as far as I know.

ANGELINA BURNETT, *Halt and Catch Fire* writer:

I'm on the board of the Writers Guild, and this actually came up in a board meeting. People keep saying culture change is hard, and that's fucking bullshit. Culture change is the easiest fucking thing we can do, and it's already changed. What's hard is structural and systemic change. That's fucking hard, but it can't even happen without cultural change.

I believe the culture has changed. Undeniably, forever the culture has changed. Now, is that change a total shift—have we just remade the fucking coastline, or have the tides shifted a little bit? I don't know which it is, and it's gonna depend on how much structural and systemic change we're able to achieve.

I can say that from my position inside the guild, I have hope that structural change is happening and that we can continue to push it, but that is a cautiously optimistic hope. I don't think it's a given. I think there is a massive amount of work to be done. I think we have to be dogged and we have to be practical and we have to be strategic and we have to be willing to compromise. We have to be willing to accept that it is totally natural and normal for men to be fucking terrified right now. We have to be willing to have that conversation and draw a line to say, "Okay, I hear you, but this line we shall not cross."

SERAPHINA BRENNAN, WB Games community manager:

I think the industry hasn't really changed that much. [Sighs] Things have gotten slightly better, but I think that was the progression we already had. I don't think there was this fundamental massive shift after Gamergate, because of that ignorance and that reluctance to engage with it in either direction. So I think gamers will be frustrated that we didn't listen to them, and on the other side, people who wanted more freedom in storytelling or creative choices didn't really get that either. We kept our core and just kept going the way we are.

Fundamentally, I haven't really seen a shift in the companies that I'd been in. I haven't heard of a shift from people I talk to. I've heard the same frustration a lot of times. I don't think we've been changed.

GINA HARA, filmmaker:

Right after Gamergate, there was a dark two years. A lot of people left the industry, a lot of people burned out, a lot of people even harmed themselves. It was really, really upsetting. It was really hard to overcome these few years after Gamergate.

I know people who left games around that time. They're not working with games anymore. They're much better now and they're healthy again. The people who stayed in games, they're doing well and they're making changes and they're doing all this cool stuff. . . . But we did lose some people who would have been possibly really great in games as well, but they just couldn't take it. It was too much.

I'm not trying to make them sound like a victim. I just don't want to hurt anyone. A lot of people got really hurt and it's their business, so I don't feel the right to talk about their experiences. It's tough because often these people, they don't want to talk about this anymore, and I think we are losing out on the people who were hurt the most, whose accounts would be the most important to listen to.

LULU LAMER, videogame producer:

It is so *deeply* ironic that tech loves to pride themselves on taking on these really hard problems when the hardest problems, wicked problems, are these complex, interrelated social, economic dynamic messes, right? Those are the ones that nobody knows how to solve, and tech is not helping because possibly the problems are too hard or I don't know. Honestly, I have no idea. Well, of course I do: There's no money in it. There's no money in solving a lot of the worst problems, the really intense problems.

MAUREEN RYAN, *Variety* **TV critic:**

This has kind of been one of my mantras the last few years: Even if you *want* to be a complete asshole, it's bad business. It's *really* bad for business. You can't just mouth the words. You have to actually put teeth behind it. Again, people act like it's just this incredibly difficult rocket science. My husband works at a bank. Things that have been said and done to me, to women that I know, if they happened at that bank, that person would be out of the building by the end of the day. They don't care. They can get more people.

The thing is, whether you're talking about gaming industries, social media companies, Silicon Valley, Hollywood studios, these are all extremely desirable jobs to get. You can scream and absolutely scream, scream however you want. Scream for not a shithead. Not a racist asshole. You think that you couldn't put up online advertising for that person's job and not get two hundred applicants by the time you went to bed? They are choosing, in many cases, to not do anything about this stuff and acting like it isn't a choice. "Well, we don't know." You do know. You could know. You don't want to.

CHAPTER 4

ALWAYS BEEN HERE,
NOT GOING ANYWHERE

Debunking the Myth of the Boys Club

VANGIE BEAL, *GameGirlz* **founder:**

Before online gaming, as a female gamer prior to that we didn't talk about gaming. When I was fifteen, sixteen, I played Atari 2600, I played Nintendo, I played Super Nintendo, and I played these games with female friends within my age group.

But we never talked about gaming. It just wasn't something we discussed. We went to each other's houses, we played the games. We didn't go to school and talk about playing games. It just was not a part of our social repertoire. . . . I don't know why. I really don't have a reason for it.

JOANNE MCNEIL, art critic/writer:

Last winter, over the holidays, my mom told me and my sister, my brother—it just came out in conversation. She said when we would go to bed, she would play Nintendo. Twenty-five years later, she was telling us that when we went to bed, she was playing *Paperboy* and *Super Mario*. [Laughs] I just keep thinking about, this is like a classic example of anybody could just play games, but there was so much identity forming or so much of this sense of who it was for or who might have fun with it that my mom, we just didn't even know. [Laughs] She didn't want to interrupt us when we're playing. My mom is not really big into pop culture.

STEPHANIE HARVEY, *Counter-Strike* **world champion:**

I've been playing games my whole life. My parents bought me consoles when I was really young. I'm thirty-two years old and I remember my six-years-old birthday party—I still have pictures. We were ten girls and we're playing *Mario Kart*. I also remember I would do sleepovers with my friends and we'd rent the Nintendo 64 and we'd just play *Wave Race 64* all night. The idea of gaming as a girl was always part of my life.

But it wasn't until I reached high school and I started going to competitions and being more involved in the *Counter-Strike* community that people were like, "Do you realize you're the only woman out of five hundred people right now?" And I'll be like, "Oh shit, I did not realize." It wasn't before other people put it in my face that I realized that. That's also when the media would start to get interested in, "Oh, you guys are a thousand people in a cafeteria playing games and there's only three women. Let's go talk to these women."

LULU LAMER, **videogame producer:**

When I started working at Looking Glass Studios [in 1998], there was an internal jargon and a whole ridiculous vocabulary of insider terms and jokes that were all intermixed with each other. Coming to get the humor and to understand the reason for the work they did and their design ethos, I really liked it. I really bought into it, and because I understood all the jokes and knew how to fit into the culture, I *belonged* in that culture.

I started working there after I had been temping at an insurance agency for like a year. [Laughs] So going into someplace where I did feel like I could fit in and that really felt creative and energetic and energized, that was great, and I totally wanted to identify with that and I grabbed on. And so I absolutely participated in the exclusionary culture that such an insular culture requires. You know, it's inward focused, therefore it keeps other people out.

The culture at Looking Glass was not specifically exclusionary to women, not at all. There were more women per capita working at Looking Glass than any other game company I've ever worked at. That was just part of the culture. The exclusionary culture was totally an intellectual inside joke. [Laughs] Not anything like the entitled manbaby gamer stuff that we see today. That was going on at the same time. It just was not happening in Cambridge, Massachusetts.

My exposure to that started when I started reading [late '90s gaming commentary site] *Old Man Murray* and [developer gossip forum] *Fatbabies* and all of those affiliated websites. There were splinter groups within that forum culture that were a lot more "Make me a sandwich." All that kind of shit. So I saw it, but it was, "Oh wow, that's weird." My exposure to the shitty toxic masculinity–type culture was through the games magazines that our games appeared in and who I had to talk to for press stuff.

MAUREEN RYAN, *Variety* **TV critic:**

I worked for Sendai Media Group, which owned [print magazine] *Electronic Gaming Monthly.* I worked at Sendai in the '90s when *EGM* every month was this big. [Gestures] The people I worked with, when I would ever talk to somebody in the gaming worlds were like, "You know Cowboy? You know this person?" I'm like, "Yeah, they're real fuckin' weird." But whatever. That's where I have some of my insight into that culture, because there were a hundred people working there and I was the third woman because they decided to have a consumer-forward TV and film magazine. I was one of the editors there. That was a trip. I remember hiring women because I wanted to not be one of the only ones. [Laughs]

There was this big bullpen where a lot of people had their cubes or offices or whatever. You'd have to walk through it to get to the vending machines and sometimes we just went around a different way to not go through that. Imagine you're in a bullpen of forty gamers and you're a young woman walking through there just wanting some Fritos. It was fucking weird. Some people were totally nice and friendly and great, but it was not welcoming. [Laughs] It was just weird and creepy.

STEPHANIE HARVEY, *Counter-Strike* **world champion:**

It was more the events and the media that made me feel like *I* was different at first. When online became bigger, that's when the community also made me feel like I was different. [Laughs] Before there was a lot of online communities, and it was local, in Québec I felt pretty normal. I didn't feel different and it felt great. I was never put into this situation where I couldn't do certain things because of my gender before I started going to tournaments for *Counter-Strike* and people started telling me I was the only girl playing. I was playing with girls my whole life before that. It wasn't weird or anything.

VANGIE BEAL, *GameGirlz* **founder:**

[The marginalization] came from both media and gamers in the community. I remember actually back to some of the first interviews I did, some of the questions like, "Do you feel like a drag king when you play?" And I'm like, "Pardon me?" [Laughs] This is a *journalist* asking me, and I'm like, "Did you *really* just ask me that?" So for me that was a bit of a surprise. I really had not expected that.

One of the original interviews we did as a female gaming group was with *Wired* magazine and they did a great photo—I guess the media turned it into a little more aggressive than what we had set out to be. Some of the quotes were maybe out of context more than others.

CHRIS KRAMER, videogame publicist:

Go back and look at the first interviews with [game producer and executive] Jade Raymond. When Jade first came on the scene in the games industry [in the late '90s]: very smart woman, very good-looking. The videogame media didn't know what to do with themselves. Lots of embarrassing shit, like "articles" about how her hair smelled. [Sighs]

I'm telling you, honestly, I sat through presentations all the way through the early 2000s where whatever game I was working on at whatever company I was at, the primary target was men age eighteen to twenty-seven of just about every videogame I ever worked on. That was the primary group 'cause that was identified as who the gaming audience was.

AL LOWE, *Leisure Suit Larry* **creator:**

I've been contacted over the years by tens of thousands of people who have played my games, so I kinda have a picture of those people. We had no market research at the time. We knew nothing about who was buying the games or why. However, we did get registration cards back from people and it was surprising because [adult-themed game] *Leisure Suit Larry* ran between a quarter and a third women.

Everybody was surprised at that. Everybody thought it was a guys-only game. But I think what happened was that women, when they tried it, they realized that I was making fun of men. The women were always superior in the games, and there weren't a lot of games like that out back then. [Laughs]

It was a real schizophrenic project because on the one hand, I'm trying to promote this misogynistic, offensive character, but the way I went about balancing it was to make the women always smarter and quicker and more intelligent and just more with it. So partly that helped me make fun of Larry, but it also balanced the game so there was . . . It wasn't misogynistic, as the box seemed to make it. If you looked at the box, you probably wouldn't think it was anything but a misogynistic sausage fest, but the box was always much dirtier than the game itself.

CHRIS KRAMER, videogame publicist:

I think historically if you look back to the dawn of home video-games, videogames used to be stigmatized. They weren't this global phenomenon. You didn't have fifty million people playing *Apex Legends* in the '90s. You had maybe a million people playing *Mario Bros.* or *Super Mario Bros.* or *Super Mario World*, whatever. One of the *Marios*. A really big game sold maybe a million units, and that was the hugest game ever. And there definitely was a perception that videogaming was a very nerdy hobby of the *Warcraft* guy in the basement with pizza on his face and no hope of ever meeting a woman. That was *a hundred percent* the perception.

STEVE KENT, journalist:

What happened is guys were naturally attracted to [gaming]. Computers in the '70s attracted nerdy guys and a small handful of nerdy women or nerdy girls, but it was really a much smaller handful. This was something that guys were interested in. In all fairness, society had been telling "Boys, you'll be doing this. Girls, you'll be doing that." For the longest time, girls had been relegated to Barbies, and boys who couldn't do sports did things other than sports.

We definitely were reporting on the bias. The gaming media sheep-ishly had to admit it was there. If you're Arnie Katz publishing *Electronic Games* or you're any of the big outlets—*Game Informer*—in the '90s, you're not really in a rush to point out problems with the game indus-try. You're just trying to celebrate what's there. They were reacting to complaints, but Sega even started, of course, to try and get girls playing. This was the mid-'90s, more in the middle.

They had this great commercial, Sega did. It was by the same people who did those other, you know, the Sega scream commercials. They had one where it showed these little girls and they're like, "So and so got this new Barbie," and you see this little herd of girls going in time-lapse photography, you see her go to the one house and then they go, "And so and so got the new Barbie dream car." You see the herd go to the next house. "And so and so got the new plushie this or that." The herd goes to that house. And then they go, "So and so got the Sega Genesis." And they list some games that were more girl-friendly and the herd goes there and then you hear, "And so and so got this toy." And nobody leaves the house with the Genesis. And then, of course, it finished with the Sega scream as always. It was a good commercial. I don't think that that ever took off, though. I'm not sure that in the end they ran the commercial on TV.

JENNY HANIVER, *Not in the Kitchen Anymore* **founder:**

What I've run into personally is the attitude that: "Well, I earned the right to be here. I had this interest when it wasn't cool and I was made fun of for it. I was called a nerd. I was called a loser. People made fun of me, but I stuck with it 'cause I was passionate about gaming and now all of these people . . . "—and it's usually pointed at women, because the trope is women don't play videogames.

So they're saying, "You don't even like it. You're doing it to impress men, you're doing it to impress your boyfriend, you're doing it to be cool because it's more socially acceptable now." That's the going nar-rative that I've always heard.

BEN FRITZ, *Wall Street Journal* **bureau chief:**

When the first PlayStation came out, there was a commercial for it [in 1998] that showed a guy locking his girlfriend in a closet so he could play the games. I don't know if that's where you can mark the beginning of misogynistic game culture to that point, but it seems like it's early on and it seems like it's a very potent example of the idea that: "It's for us, it's not for them, and it's just something we do without them and something that they'll never understand. We have to keep it away from them because they won't want us to do it. They won't let us have our fun. This is our thing, it's not theirs."

That becomes a loop, "It's not for them," and the more it's not for them, the more it's gonna be stuff that would be unappealing to or offensive to women. Ultra-violence, portraying women as objects, etc., not having very many, if any, female protagonists and when you do you get the bad versions: Lara Croft. That becomes a bad self-fulfilling prophecy.

CHRIS MANCIL, EA global director of community:

Fundamentally, the marketing side was . . . It all comes back to the business. Even twenty years ago, companies were very . . . We knew who was buying the game or not. If you know who is most likely to buy your game, you can serve advertising that titillates and engages and excites them pretty easily. Now if you're good, if you're a good marketer, if you're smart, you tell great stories. You can make great campaigns that make you feel good about a product and really showcase the features of your game and why it's different and why it's something that you should care about and why it's worth your time.

Unfortunately, not everyone is great at marketing, and there's a lot of cheap ways and easy ways to get there. You can sexualize and objectivize women. You can use sex to sell. You can use grotesque violence, you can use juvenile humor, you can use a lot of things that are shortcuts to get you the attention that you want that may get you the results you're looking for. Fundamentally, at the end of the day, it is about results. It's true in any industry, certainly true for videogames. The marketplace is going to pick who wins and loses, and that's ultimately consumers buying games. There were lots of games that would oversize the anatomy of girls to appeal to a certain demo. There were ones who would use grotesque violence or shocking things just to get attention.

But I would say that the games industry isn't like that anymore, at least not in the West. It always started with "We know who wants to buy this game or who's the highest percentage likely to buy this game, and with your limited dollars what's the most effective way to maximize that target audience?" That was the historical way of thinking about it. There were good ways to do it and there were shortcut ways to do it. . . . That led to a lot of excesses, but I think those excesses weren't necessarily market driven. I'm convinced those excesses were due to talent less than a conspiracy against women. This is maybe being generous, but I just think that people who weren't good at marketing and just shouldn't be in the business always chose the easiest base emotions to get where we needed to go.

CHRIS KRAMER, videogame publicist:

When I came into the games industry in the early '90s, videogames were kind of shameful. A lot of the marketing people I knew were just passing through videogames and would greenlight marketing campaigns that have very little to do about the game but had suggestive sexual material. If you look back at the UK games marketing in the '90s, oh my God, it was horrendous. It was as many half-naked women as they could fit into a page in a magazine. The idea was, "Oh, it's just teenage and early twenties boys who are playing these games, and they're dorks, so we're going to try and titillate 'em and grab their attention with boobs."

When I was talking about people who are just passing through the games industry, I was thinking in particular of the TV ad that was produced for *Street Fighter Alpha* on PlayStation One [in 1996]. The whole gist of the *hilarious* commercial was that there's a teenage boy who appears to be masturbating in his darkened bedroom while watching a video and his mom walks in on him and she was like, "Oh, Johnny!" And he's like, "Oh, Mom! Get out!" The camera pulls back and he doesn't have his pants down. He's holding onto a fight stick and playing *Street Fighter* and, ha ha, isn't that hilarious?

There were a group of us at Capcom at that time who were *fucking* incensed at that commercial. We were like, "How are you spending money on this? This is ridiculous." There are a bunch of guys in our early twenties who are actual gamers talking to the marketing experts who are people in their thirties and forties—so they were hella older than us—and I remember saying, "You're making fun of the people that you want to buy this game." And they just didn't get it. They're like, "No, this is really funny. It's gonna play well."

STEVE KENT, journalist:

I think that more boys played videogames than girls. I think boys were more interested in videogames. Right now, and if we're being honest, if you were to go to Scholastic or some other publisher and get internal numbers, you'd probably see that more girls are reading books than boys. You just would.

LULU LAMER, videogame producer:

So when Gamergate was actually happening—I took a couple years off to have kids—I was at home hearing about all this shit on the radio and being like, "Oh, thank God I'm not there right now." Because my last job before I left [big-budget] AAA games [in 2012] was at 2K and part of the reason that I didn't feel like I had a long-term future at 2K was because there was zero interest in expanding the audience. I knew if we don't expand the audience we're not going to grow, and just finding more young to middle-age white guys or men—actually games cross racial lines a lot more than we think—but just catering to these young guys? That's not a strategy for growth.

There was a strong expectation our games would continue to grow an audience sequel after sequel. The sales expectation for *BioShock Infinite* was something like eight million [units] at the time that I worked on it. I was working on that game for a relatively short time before I went on maternity leave. The previous ones had sold, maybe it was five million? But it was a jump of three million, right, two or three million. Where are those people gonna come from? Just grappling with that was not realistic at all because we're not making new gamers out of women or people with lower-end systems or . . . I don't know. Somewhere? There's a lot of rocks to turn over, but we're not turning over any of those rocks. We're like, "Let's try to pull *Call of Duty* players." That was the marketing strategy for *Spec Ops: The Line*, which if you think about it is silly.

So yeah, a real unwillingness to engage with the need to find other kinds of games that other kinds of players would like in order to continue selling games and being profitable and meet the needs of Wall Street and their expectations of continuous growth. I can *imagine* that working at 2K. What kind of conversation were they having about Gamergate? I don't really know. I can't say. I wasn't there. But if you're not willing to really engage in a conversation about your audience . . . I always felt patronized for bringing it up: "Oh, well, that's because you're a woman and that's your little pet project, giving a shit about expanding the audience." People above me, more than one person, was saying that.

CHRIS MANCIL, EA global director of community:
Even at Ubisoft in 2001, we were having these conversations: How do we expand beyond our very hardcore demographic? I think any game maker, any game publisher, wants to be more mainstream, and Ubisoft was no exception. Back then Ubisoft was definitely an up-and-comer and growing in North America. But at the time they were pretty much known for *Rayman* and were starting to expand into the Tom Clancy world, which is definitely male-dominated, military shooters and so forth. But even then it was a huge topic of conversation, not only at Ubisoft but at game-developer conferences and throughout the industry—which was much smaller then—which is how do we make games that appeal to more than just our core demographic?

That was not only a cultural need: "We wanna be artists that appeal more to this one segment." It's also a business reality, like, "Hey, how do we grow gaming to be a bigger business? How do we become more like movies and film and television and radio?" Back then it was radio. "How do we become more of a mainstream type of media?" It's hilarious now because I haven't really thought about it much since then, but we had a little chip on our shoulder back then. We were like, "Hey, we're this new growing entertainment space." But back then people would laugh at us, compared to movies or television.

The best way I've ever heard it said was that the problem was we were pretty good at building games we knew lots of boys would want to play . . . We really did want to make games for more than just boys. But that's all philosophical. All the conspiracy theories aside, the reality was this is economics driven, and the fact was boys wanted to play games and they wanted to buy games.

CHRIS KRAMER, videogame publicist:

Self-reflection isn't a strong point of any industry and it definitely helps when other people hold mirrors up to it. . . . Because of the boys-club nature of the games industry at that point in time, anytime there was anything involving a woman or women, they would latch onto it because it was seen as almost strange. Like, "What is this visitor from another planet that seems to have different chromosomes than I do? I don't understand." So, you can look back, like when Ubisoft started promoting the Frag Dolls,* like the Frag Dolls could barely play *Quake* for the most part. But it was a bunch of good-looking girls that they could trot out and go, "Oh, look at our women who plays videogames, boys! Come cover this." It seemed very cynical at the time.

The media was, to a certain extent—by reporting on things like Frag Dolls, or how unusual it was to see women involved in the games industry—I think it was definitely reinforcing the stereotype unintentionally. Even when there were people who were trying to help elevate the role of women in the games industry just by constantly reporting on how unusual it was, or, "Look at this over here," it was only reinforcing the narrative of, "Well, women don't really do this, except for this one person over here."

MICHAEL WILSON, cosplayer:

Everyone knew it was happening. Everyone knew it was there, sexism, racism. But it was almost taboo to talk about it. If you were the one to bring it up and acknowledge it, then you were the one that's, I don't know, almost trying to take the fun out of everything. You're like the Debbie Downer of the group. . . . I honestly want to say it's equally racist, but I think the sexism is worse.

HARRY DENHOLM, *No Man's Sky* senior programmer:

From my point of view, so many more people play videogames now that how could we not have a broader selection of personalities in this space?

---

* Initially formed in 2004 by videogame publisher Ubisoft, the Frag Dolls were a group of professional female gamers recruited and employed to promote Ubisoft's games, including participation in esports tournaments. The name refers to three different teams in the United States, the United Kingdom, and France. The Frag Dolls dissolved in 2015.

LISA NAKAMURA, gender and technology researcher:

I was watching the [2016] *Overwatch* league controversy around the first female pro player, who was a Korean woman named Geguri. *Overwatch* . . . [has] so many female avatars, so much ethnic diversity. They built that game for all kinds of audiences, characters that really represent the Middle East, East Asia. There's Black people, Brazilian people. They made it this rainbow of different types of people. It's amazing.

But they still have the same problems with toxicity in their game. . . . They only have one female player [in the league] and everyone thought she was cheating. Geguri had to film a video of her playing live with a camera showing her mouse hand to show she wasn't cheating 'cause people thought no girl can aim that well.

DIXON WU, Neo Geo World Tour organizer:

In particular places—in Korea, for example, or in Japan—if I were to rate them, I would say Korea might be . . . No offense to them, it's just how the culture is, right? Korea would probably be one of these places where men dominate. Like, they would have to just tell you that they dominate. They feel offended when they get beat, especially in a game, they get beaten by a girl for example. They get very offended because then their friends would laugh at them. "Oh, you got beaten by a girl." I went to Korea and I've seen a husband slap their wife [over a videogame] in a restaurant in front of everyone. If you translate that into gaming, traditionally gaming has always been male dominant. So if girls just love videogames and they try to get into it, they will naturally get rejected.

KATIE FLEMING, *Katie's Tomb Raider Site* founder:

[Harassment] never happened with *Tomb Raider*, but if I was playing any other online games, as soon as they saw a girl's name in the room obviously they knew I was a girl and of course you always get comments like, "Oh my God, are you really a girl?," or, "Girls don't play games," or, "Show me your boobs." Anything and everything. Just stupid shit. And I remember always being like, "Who gives a crap if you're a guy or a girl? You're playing a game. You're there to have fun." I never fed into it honestly because I just thought it was so stupid to begin with. Like, I'm not gonna sit there typing insults back and forth if I'm there to go shoot things. [Laughs]

ALBA, videogame streamer:

I've always been kind of mouthy. [Laughs] A lot of the times I feel like [male players] are testing you, which is a weird concept, and I don't know why that would be happening either. But I remember this—I came at the kid hard. [Laughs] We were all in voice, I think six people were. He said something like, "Oh my God, are you a girl?!" And I was like, "Oh my God, are you a virgin?!" And then everyone busted out laughing, and there was no toxicity for the rest of the game and it was just chill.

I think they're afraid they'd have to put on airs if females entered the community, and this is a place where they don't want to do that. I never really thought about the psychology of it, but a lot of times in my experience if you say something smart back, they'll be like, "All right, all right." They're testing to see if you're going to . . . I don't know, they assume girls will freak out over any little thing. And then there's people who just, no, relentlessly seem to have a very big vendetta against women.

ANGELINA BURNETT, *Halt and Catch Fire* writer:

I hadn't thought about this in so long. [In 1998] I used to play Yahoo! Spades and Canasta. I used to have a group of friends who I'd play cards with all the time in high school, and then when I was in college and then I moved away and I didn't have that group anymore I was like, "Oh shit, I can play cards online, this is so great!" Those are both partner games and so you would partner up with a stranger, a faceless stranger.

I remember making a stupid move and just getting absolutely berated, ripped to fucking shreds, and then the partner force-quit the game, forfeiting. It was like, "Cunt, fucking bitch." Whatever it was. And I was like, "Woah! I made a bad move. I'm really sorry, but it's a card game!" [Laughs]

LISA NAKAMURA, gender and technology researcher:

Anger on the internet generally escalates much more quickly than face-to-face environments. I had lots of scholars ask me, "Do you think that racism is so intense with gaming on the internet because it's a competitive environment or because it's an environment where people's adrenaline gets worked up? They're trying to shoot something or be shot." And I had these great screenshots from *Words with Friends* where people talk to each other, "Suck my dick." [Laughs] So no, I don't think it has to do with the content of the game! You'll find trolling and harassment in *any* kind of game.

RICH WEIL, *FusionFall* community manager:

I don't think that just because somebody doesn't yet know the proper way to treat people, whether they're men or women or what-ever, I don't think that necessarily makes them a bad person. Some-times it just makes them young and they just haven't learned yet. The gaming spectrum skews young male. I'm not telling you any news. It's no surprise that when people could interact with other people that that came out.

I've talked to people since then, people who were horrible people online back in *Ultima Online* or *EverQuest*, and now they're like, "Wow, I was terrible. I was a terrible person." So I do think there's capacity for change. That's vastly different than what the Gamergate and incel★ wackos are doing now. It's apples and oranges, really, and I have no sympathy in any way for that stuff.

JENNY HANIVER, *Not in the Kitchen Anymore* founder:

It's not just teenagers. My website is a perfect example, because if you listen to the clips you can tell that they're very clearly by and large not teenagers just by the sound of their voices. It's primarily men

---

★ Incels, short for "involuntary celibates," compose inceldom, an online subculture characterized by individuals who identify as unable to find romantic or sexual partners despite a desire to do so. The term has gained attention for its association with toxic ideologies, misogyny, and a sense of resentment toward those perceived as "more successful" in romantic relationships. Both "incel" and "inceldom" are derived from "invcel," which was first coined in the mid-'90s by a queer Canadian student known as Alana with her website Alana's Involuntary Celibacy Project. In 2018 she told the BBC that the site was a "friendly" and "supportive place" for men and women to talk about being lonely. While many self-identified incels do not engage in violence, there have been several high-profile incidents where individuals who identified with the incel community carried out violent attacks.

who I believe are anywhere from their mid-twenties or early twenties to late thirties.

The one that always sticks out to me was, I had a guy who after a match—I think my team beat his—he sent me a voicemail [through Xbox] saying he was gonna impregnate me and then force me to have a late-term abortion with strict mental abuse, and then he giggled. [Laughs] It was like, all right, this is a videogame and you're basically saying you want to rape someone and make them have an abortion. And it's just like, what? I can't understand what world people are living in where this is fun to them.

VANGIE BEAL, *GameGirlz* founder:

I got a letter in the mail [in 1999] that was absolutely horrendous and it scared me because I'm in little rural Nova Scotia, Canada. I have no clue how this person even got my mailing address, and it was an awful letter that really called me out for being an awful mother because I was a female and I played games and I had a child. And at that point I was just like, "I think I've run my course." I was done. It kind of just hit me: I can still be a gamer, but I can actually have fun with this if I'm not doing the public voice. That was the turning point for me.

LISA NAKAMURA, gender and technology researcher:

A lot of people say, "I opt out. I don't identify as a gamer. I'll play, but I will never use the headset. I've just seen what happens to women, so I'm just not going to be part of the culture." That's really bad because it makes the balance of power even worse than it already is.

So, I think gaming culture has an opportunity. There's plenty of women playing, but the atmosphere has gotten so chilled because of Gamergate that people aren't willing to even try to engage. Something needs to happen.

ANGELINA BURNETT, *Halt and Catch Fire* writer:

Okay, this is really simple, man: patriarchy. I don't wanna go fucking gender studies on you. . . . Of course a new exciting technology that builds economic viability and makes a lot of money for people, of course it's going to be the purview for men because everything is the fucking purview for men. I don't think games are special. [Laughs] I mean, that's the answer.

GRACE, *Fat, Ugly, or Slutty?* **cofounder:**

We got so many emails unprompted from men just emailing us to apologize for men. There was just like a whole bunch of them that they just had to write in and apologize for men. You even see this in replies on Twitter now, somebody posts something and they're like, "Oh my God, on behalf of all men, I am so fucking ashamed. I'm so sorry." There's this weird tension, but if there's something that's happening with women, I'm not hearing about it. And so you gotta go back to: What are we teaching men?

RICH WEIL, *FusionFall* **community manager:**

The impression that the game industry is overrun with toxicity is not entirely accurate. I think that a lot of that is because of the attention that's been paid to those people. If I was God-emperor of the world and/or I could make everybody do exactly what I wanted them to do I would . . . My strategy would be nobody give these guys a platform. Meanwhile we'll aggressively go after them. We'll make sure we control the message and expose them, publish who they are, and publish what they say. But in the meantime, we're not going to write article after article after article after article about it and give them the publicity that they so desperately crave. That would be probably the way I would do it, but that's impossible.

I go to almost every PAX.* I go to almost every one every year. I don't go to the Australia one, but I'm working on my boss with that one. I go to PAX South, I go to PAX East, I go to PAX West. I go every year. I've been doing that for five years now. Three shows a year, fifteen times I've been to PAX shows. I never see anything but people having fun, a very diverse crowd, people being nice to each other, and just having a good time. That's the game industry right there.

---

* A series of gaming culture festivals associated with the videogame-oriented web comic *Penny Arcade*. PAX is held annually in various locations, including Seattle, Boston, Philadelphia, and Melbourne.

I don't see guys picketing the Blizzard booth or whatever because they hired a female developer. You don't see that stuff in real life. It's almost practically a political argument, which is harmful because they do apparently have a significant megaphone or at least they've been given a significant megaphone. But I think it's completely off-base to say that toxicity has taken over the game industry because I just don't see it.

If I went to PAX and I saw people getting into fights and I saw people picketing and I saw people turning over tables at booths because they hated that there were women manning the booth and stuff like that, then I would say, "Yeah, okay. We got some serious, serious problems. This problem is *huge*."

JENNY HANIVER, *Not in the Kitchen Anymore* **founder:**

We already know this is a thing. We have all these examples. We know it's bad. I think the next step is pointing out that this is not just good-natured trolling, because that's what it gets dismissed as: "It's trolling." Well, no. You have people who are honestly making murder threats or rape threats towards other users. Are they actually going to find that person's house, drive there, and kill them? Probably not. But swatting has become a very real, weird thing. It needs to be taken seriously and it needs to not be just dismissed because people need to realize like, yeah, you *can* say stuff, but there are repercussions or there should be repercussions.

MAUREEN RYAN, *Variety* **TV critic:**

You can't be a free-speech absolutist. No company is a free-speech absolutist. If you walked up to the CEO's house and painted a swastika on it, you would get fired. No one's an absolutist in these matters except for stuff that they would rather ignore.

ANGELINA BURNETT, *Halt and Catch Fire* **writer:**

You can accept culpability without being morally repugnant. We have put these labels, like, "You're a racist." Suddenly it's the worst fucking thing you could be when in reality, it's really fuckin' human to be tribal. If you could just acknowledge your biases and your shortcomings, you can begin to confront them. Everyone's fucking got them.

All of us are broken imperfect human beings hopefully doing the best we can. Let's start from that place and then move forward.

AARON BLEYAERT, *Conan* **senior digital producer:**

I don't think it's limited to videogames. It's symptomatic of a much larger problem with society and how people are communicating and mutual respect. Videogames are getting a larger and larger slice of the culture pie and the entertainment pie, and with that comes this stuff that is happening with the rest of society and culture unfortunately. It's a real shame and it's important for people to be proactive in that.

We all have a responsibility to do what's right, and we all have a responsibility when you see something that's not right to do something and say something about it, because otherwise it doesn't stop. I just think that's a general note, not just for videogames but for life in general. You should live your life. We should all be kind to each other. It's trite, but it's true, right? But, unfortunately, not followed often enough. Easier said than done, but better done than only said. I wouldn't say it's a videogame problem. I think it's a societal problem and a big one at that. Like, what the fuck man? Like, Jesus Christ, can we just all love each other and play videogames? Is that *that* hard?

CHAPTER 5

STAY THE FUCK OUT OF IT

Fandom and Gatekeeping

LISA NAKAMURA, gender and technology researcher:
I think the relationship between the game industry and its fans is *way* more complicated than it is between any other media industry and its fans because it's such a porous border between being a modder, a player, a pro, a developer. People move in and out of those roles, and they want to move in and out of those roles.

Gamers invest so much time, they feel entitlement in a way that movie fans would never dare to feel. You don't invest all this time in movies, but additionally you don't have this porous boundary of "Oh, I can be in that movie." There's no way you're going to be in this Miramax movie. [Laughs] That's not gonna happen.

So you have this respect for your role, which is as an audience member. But I see game fans often invoke retail rights. Like, "We pay for this, you owe us X." That is not typical of other media fandoms either. You don't have a permanent seat at the table to criticize films because you bought a ticket. So disrupting that kind of stuff? Where it came from? I don't know. But I think that is also a form of symbolic ownership, which is unique to games and their fans.

HOWARD CHAYKIN, cartoonist:
Anecdotally, many years ago, I was at a comic-book convention. I was a guest on a panel. The panel was discussing the concept of mini-series when such things were new, and one of the attendees raised the

issue that they didn't like miniseries because the stories would end before they had an opportunity to write letters to impact in some way the conclusion or the narrative, which blindsided me because when did this ever become a democracy? That's just nonsense.

SERAPHINA BRENNAN, WB Games community manager:

One of my coworkers received a threat from a person, a player, who we knew was very much an invested player who spent a lot of money on the game and had a lot of money. He sent a death threat attached with a [copy of a] plane ticket and instructions of how to get to our office saying, "I'm coming," which was immediately passed off to the appropriate authorities and they took it very seriously. They said, "Okay, this guy clearly has the funds." They actually went to him before he left. I'm not sure what happened there, but they interacted with him in some way before he even got on his flight.

But just to be sure, we attached a security detail to my coworker. So not only were they sitting in front of their office all day just in case, but they actually walked him to his car every day after work for about two weeks. It was attached to *Dungeons & Dragons Online*, and it happened in 2014. . . . It was over just a disagreement on the forums, if I remember correctly. He just believed that my coworker insulted him in some way or just demeaned him and he wanted to get rid of him in the worst way possible.

But to ask how we got there, it's hard to pinpoint where this anger began to boil over. I would say when we started offering more connectivity, in the early days of massively multiplayer games. They were, in my mind, the forerunners for a lot of this because they're the first games that started patching themselves and changing. They also offered forums and chat rooms to really connect staff members with players. I think that was a unique aspect of gaming that you didn't see in other forms of entertainment.

SOREN JOHNSON, *Civilization IV* lead designer:

I feel like I always heard the MMO* guys talk about [threats] happening to them a long time back. But I was definitely not working on

---

* Massively multiplayer online games are virtual worlds that support large numbers of simultaneous players, *World of Warcraft* being one of the most successful, by far.

online games, so I didn't experience that much myself. My guess is that as it became more prevalent, the more games moved to becoming a service, as opposed to becoming a single project where you get it and: "Well, this is a box. If I don't like it, too bad. It's not going to change. It's a physical object." Obviously there's patches but it's just a different feel, as opposed to something where especially if you're paying monthly, that's obviously where people would get the most aggravated.

SERAPHINA BRENNAN, WB Games community manager:
A staff member from Marvel Comics or DC isn't going to drop by a forum and be like, "Hey guys, what do you think of the latest Batman?" They can't fix the Batman. With a movie, Zack Snyder isn't going to drop by a chat room and be like, "Hey, how could I fix my next movie?" But with gaming, we're very connected with the people that we are actively providing entertainment to because we are an ongoing product.

So I would say it's definitely the rise of live services that began this rise of personal toxicity and vitriol that seems to have permeated, because we broke down those barriers ourselves. We wanted to break down those barriers. We wanted to make our games better and we wanted people to have fun, but in return, because those barriers were now gone, people got emboldened and they thought that they can demand things of us. They can scream and yell and stomp their feet and in some cases take it one step further to those death threats and then take advantage of scare tactics to essentially get us to change something about the game.

RICHARD BARTLE, online game pioneer/researcher:
I mean, I had death threats in my time, but none of them were credible. But if you get fifty a day, then it starts to be a little more worrying.

AL LOWE, *Leisure Suit Larry* creator:
Threats? No, but if they had come in, I would've just ignored it. That accomplishes nothing. Constructive criticism or objective criticism? That's fine. Threats? No, that's ridiculous.

DAVID DEWALD, BioWare community manager:
In 2007, 2006? I got doxed back then. We were cracking down on bad behavior in the *9Dragons* community. . . . At one point they tried

to post my address online, and it just so happened that where I was living, even though David DeWald isn't a very common name, there happened to be a David DeWald that owned property in the city I lived in, but I did not. They put his name and address on Blogger, of all places.

So I contacted Blogger and said, "I just want you to know that this is part of a greater problem in that this person has tried to dox me by publishing stuff online. However, it is not accurate information and I would like you to remove it so that this person doesn't have somebody show up on his front porch screaming about a videogame and he has no idea what's going on." And they said at the time that it was factual information so they would not remove it, because it was on public record. I actually had to prove that I did not live there so that they would know that it was *not* factual information and they would be able to remove it.

CHRIS MANCIL, EA global director of community:
I think when you get kids away from parents . . . I mean, now we're a little more smart, but there were kids that were threatening to *kill* people. I got a death threat—this is a story I share with some of my employees. Now, it's way more serious if you get a death threat. But around 2001, 2002, I used to get death threats all the time and I would just laugh it off. I would be like, literally, "That's just some kid blowing off steam on the forums." And I remember I had a boss that took it seriously and got the FBI involved, and the police identified IP addresses. I didn't know anything was happening. I learned later.

The story ended up where they found out where some of these threats against me were coming. Like, I remember one of them was: "You're gonna get off work and you're gonna walk out of the building and I'm gonna shoot you in the head. I'll be there waiting." And I was like, "Whatever." Of course, I was young, too, so I didn't really put much credence in it. But when they tracked the IP down—I think it was a house in North Carolina or somewhere like that—and the FBI director and I think local law enforcement actually showed up and knocked on the house and a grandmother opened the door, and literally it was like a nine- or ten-year-old kid who tried to hide under the bed when the police showed up to ask about it. For me, it sort of personifies where we were back then, where there were people online who just didn't think this was real and just think that they could say whatever they wanted without any type of consequence or repercussion. They just didn't know better. I think a lot of them just didn't know better.

WAGNER JAMES AU, journalist/Second Life historian:

Literal death threats. I've been to game companies—[in 2012] I was at one called Kixeye where they literally had a giant bald-headed guy, military fatigues, with a Desert Eagle pistol strapped outside. He was a security guard. I asked the CEO, "What are you guys . . . Is that just for show?" He's like, "No, we've actually had people show up and make death threats." If developers do something with a game that sufficiently enrages a portion of the hardcore user base, they will actually get terrorist threats. [Laughs] That is something that they've not dealt with much.

I think for a long time the game industry has had a simultaneous self-esteem issue where they think they're less central to the culture than movies or books or TV. And then also the game developers are usually gamers themselves, so they're really invested in game-fan culture and they don't like to be seen as trashing it. I thought about this when Gamergate happened. If, for example, [Valve cofounder] Gabe Newell and a few other really well-known game developers stood up and publicly said, "Gamergate is horrible. If we catch anyone on our message board promoting it, they will get instantly banned. We don't want this. We want women in our games. We want minorities in our games and we are going to actively go after people who are against that and drive them out of our community," I think it would have ended.

I think the history might have been different if it had been nipped in the bud, because so much about gamer culture is this feeling of resentment to the outside. But it's also about gamer gods and these figures that are really admired. You can see that in message boards, if a well-respected game designer or game developer says something, then you get a large part of the community start defending them, adding value to their cause. If the industry leaders that are respected most by the community had come forward, I think it really could have gotten preempted. There was a terror in the industry to say anything. They just didn't want to say anything at all for a long time, or [they said] something really generic. Now it seems like there's less tolerance for intolerance, but right at that point, the industry had really not decided how important it was and didn't want to take ownership over this bad culture that they allowed to fester.

CHUCK KLOSTERMAN, author/pop-culture essayist:
   I'm not sure there is any subculture that does not perceive itself as persecuted and oppressed. I can't think of one. That's why people become part of groups or identify with groups. So, yesterday they announced all the people who are getting into the Rock & Roll Hall of Fame. I was listening to it on SiriusXM radio 'cause they had the announcement. There were people on the radio going, "Oh, it's so great that Roxy Music got in because this is validation for all the kids who were getting beat up by Van Halen fans." And then someone else said, "Well, but Def Leppard got in. Def Leppard, they're more like Van Halen than Roxy Music." And then they were like, "Oh, but the guys in Def Leppard *liked* Roxy Music and liked David Bowie. They probably got beat up for that." This false belief that on playgrounds across the world there was just a bloodbath going on over musical tastes.
   I'm a KISS fan, right? So all these people, when I meet KISS fans, they're always telling me how they were just harassed and teased for liking KISS. I don't remember that ever happening *ever*, once. There is a documentary called *Salad Days* about the early DC punk scene, and fifteen minutes of the documentary is about how they used to get beat up all the time and they had to do all these things to escape people driving by in Camaros and jumping out and attacking them. It just seems like if you're part of the subculture, part of being in the subculture is this idea that we are together because we are being oppressed. The people who play videogames, they think they're being oppressed for liking videogames. Then there's the people who are saying, "Oh no, we're being shut out from that world. It's this sexist world we can't participate in." They're also oppressed. Everyone's oppressed. [Laughs] Everybody involved is working from the idea that they're being stopped from doing what they want to do.

JOANNE MCNEIL, art critic/writer:
   Tech companies use this language about this sense of stigma. I mean, you find that in a lot of [entrepreneur] Peter Thiel's interviews

and his books as well, where he sees himself as a scapegoat. That's another example of people who don't want to be held accountable for their own behavior and views—it becomes being a hater. You find that in the Y Combinator [venture capital] community too. It's just that sense of, "How dare people hold you accountable? How dare people notice that you have power over them?" This is where we get a lot of conversations about outrage on the internet, when actually a lot of the time what people are calling outrage is a community of people pointing out that someone with power is acting improperly.

FLOURISH KLINK, *Fansplaining* cohost:

Who is empowered to make what decisions about what to do within this space and what are the possible consequences? Although the games industry is much more forward-looking in the sense of engaging with players and talking with them and interacting with them—partially because they have to because it's an interactive medium—there's still customary ways that people interact. [There are] concerns about over-stepping the boundaries, the consequences to an individual employee who—ultimately it is going to be mostly one employee—is champion-ing the idea. I think it's very unlikely that you're gonna have a game company just as a group being like, "Oh yes, of course we should step in!"

In order to make a decision on the spot, it's gonna ultimately be a person who is making that call, and if they step the wrong way, if they decide to chastise a user, we've seen what happens. Everyone goes, "Oh, you shouldn't have done that!" They get fired. The prob-lem continues. [Laughs] When we see this happening within films it's far worse because within films, so often, social media is so heavily controlled that there's absolutely no room for any kind of response or conversation, certainly, on the official channel. Maybe on people's private channels, but then, again, it has to be a director or somebody deciding to step in and feeling confident that they have enough power to do that and not be fired.

ALEX HUTCHINSON, Ubisoft creative director:

I think publishers just wanna hype [games] up as much as possible and they don't necessarily see the punishment that the teams can get because they never really own it. Your producers in a big studio or the management in a big studio, it's not really their game. It's your game on the team, but for them it's dollars in one column, reviews in another column. They would like it to be positively received and they would like it to make a lot of money obviously, but if you get hassled, it's not something that bothers them that much. I think they would say, "You've angled your whole career to get this job and you're a public figure now. This comes with the territory."

RAWN SHAH, *Playing MUDs on the Internet* **coauthor:**

Without any particular company in mind, there is not necessarily the recognition or the impact of social interests in the environment at the financial leadership level of the company. The game will be the game. It will behave the way it is. "We're not there to morally decide what it is." The moral cop-out where it says, "Okay, as long as you're not abusing the terms of the system itself, then go ahead and do what you want." There is no judicial system in the games or anything like that. Resolving some of those issues sometimes tend to be very simple and quick. . . . They're there to just get it done and off. It's a call-center kind of environment more than anything else.

Very often they're also under-supported. The community managers may be very interested in being able to do that, but now the games are on the scales of millions of people. There's just not enough people to handle all the situations. They're overworked. They are not prepared to handle these kinds of situations. So add to that the speed and velocity of how these toxic events happen. By the time you get to attending to this and answer the question "Should I tend to this?," it has already spiraled out of control. And once it's spiraled out of control, you get all the trolls and other folks jumping in who are there for the fun of it.

STEVE JONES, **internet researcher/professor:**

There's a piling on that happens with any phenomenon. . . . If your thing happens to be going after somebody . . . I mean, it's not unheard of with bullying behavior to see other bullies pile on when they see somebody bully somebody else. So that's not really a huge surprise.

I think to me the greater surprise is that, really, there are that many people who want to engage in that sort of behavior. What does one get out of engaging in that behavior? This is really something that you get off on? That's pretty creepy. It's a big world. There's a lot of cool stuff out there. Shitting on people shouldn't be some top priority. There's gotta be other things. Go get high or something.

RICHARD BARTLE, online game pioneer/researcher:

Back in the day if somebody was misbehaving, you got onto their university or whoever else it was and said, "Can you stop this person from doing that?" And then they'd have a word with them and if they didn't stop then they just got kicked off what would later be called the internet. Most of the people there were open-minded scientists, computer scientists. They had a hacker ethic which is computers are a force for good and a chaotic good. They used *Dungeons & Dragons* terms. So they were good, but they didn't really want to bow to authority, people telling them things that they didn't believe. So there was some . . . I wouldn't say anarchy, but it was like a freedom. There was a freedom about it and the people who were involved all played by the rules because they themselves made the rules.

In *MUD*,* we did get people coming in. We did used to get, like, fifteen-year-old schoolboys who were renowned for "Oh, what are the social boundaries of this game? Let me say 'fuck' a couple of times and find out." Well, they didn't get to say it a couple of times 'cause the first time they said it they were killed in the game. We had a finger-of-death command, and if a wizard saw you do something like that or a witch saw you do that, then they would just kill your character and that was that. *Bye-bye.*

These days if people misbehave in a game, then they're banned temporarily for a few days. Doesn't really matter. They've got other characters, they're not paying any money anyway, what do they care? So yeah, even if you're kicked off for two weeks, you're only banned. You've not been banned permanently for good just because of this one

---

* A game that also shares a name with the genre it helped to create: multi-user dungeon. Emerging in the 1970s, these early text-based multiplayer online games played a defining role in shaping the concept of online gaming, social interaction, and collaborative storytelling. *MUD* was developed by Roy Trubshaw in collaboration with Bartle in 1978 at the University of Essex.

little mistake. Well, no, you *should* be banned for good. You should just be kicked off. There are plenty of other games. Go somewhere else. We'll probably find that the same people would be banned by every game.

But that's not something which is believed to be acceptable to the gaming public. Well, okay, maybe it isn't acceptable to 10 percent, but if you get rid of those 10 percent then that 90 percent's not going to leave afterwards. Making the money that nine people give you is a bit better than the money one person gives you. And you don't want people driven away by obnoxious behavior, and also you shouldn't tolerate it. It's not just even commercially—if somebody is really causing your other users distress, then you really should be standing up. You shouldn't be saying, "Oh, we will just go into our list of things to do." You should be saying, "No, you should not be doing that. That is bad. We don't want your kind here. Off you go." And that's probably a more proactive approach to it. Of course in the US you could probably be sued for that, but at least you can't in a good many other countries, denying people a service they haven't paid for.

JONATHAN COULTON, musician:
I think people get worried because these are customers that you're dealing with. So if you ban somebody from your community, you are losing a customer. You are going against that customer and that is the thing that is not at all built into the DNA of having a company and running a company. It's not compatible. So that's part of the problem.

Another part is this confusion about what is public space and what is private space. I think back to the early blogging years, there were a couple of people who I remember were like, "You know what? I am no longer allowing comments on my posts." And people would freak out and say, "How dare you. You're infringing on my free speech." And it's like, "Well, no, I'm not. This is my space and I get to do what I want with it and I don't want any comments."

It's a confusing thing. I don't think companies are great at it and I understand why: we haven't had a lot of good examples. There doesn't exist a set of norms for what is an appropriate way to manage a community. I think we're still trying to figure that out.

DAVID WEINBERGER, *The Cluetrain Manifesto* **coauthor:**

So, Disneyland has rules about what you can do and they will ask you to leave if you break them, because they have an idea of what sort of place they want Disneyland to be. But that's also true that Disneyland is a weird example because it's like a little fantasy stage living within the real stage. [Laughs] But every bar has rules. Also, every prom you've ever been to has a set of rules for behavior based upon its idea of what sort of place it wants to be. Every restaurant, some of them, if you've got a toddler, will let you walk the toddler around and others will give you the side-eye or ask you to please control your infant. Some of them, you can't get in without a sports coat if you're a guy. I would say virtually every public space certainly has norms and those norms may rise to the level of explicit rules that are enforceable. So I don't think it's unusual for a public and online game to have an idea about what sort of space it wants to be and to enforce it.

It's very similar to what the so-called open platforms say and want to say: "Look, they're open platforms and they are not and cannot be in the business of controlling what people say and/or how they behave." That's just not true. They already do control, inevitably. Facebook, you have to use your real name. That may be good or bad, and actually there's complex arguments about whether it's good or bad depending on what culture you're in, but it's a decision that has purposeful and then second-order unintended consequences on how people behave. It's tied to a permanent ID, so there's some more accountability perhaps that people feel. On the other hand, the inability to have anonymous or pseudo-anonymous accounts has very direct effects in discourse in cultures where people feel at risk for what they say. It also discourages a sense of play and so forth.

It doesn't matter how one feels about those decisions. The point is they are decisions that have effects on the type of discourse. Facebook definitely has rules about posting porn. Again, I don't care which way the argument goes, the point is that they are, by rules and norms, deciding what sort of behavior they want to encourage or allow on their site. The same is true for *every* place or every comment section. There are decisions that are made about many of the same parameters. Can you be anonymous or pseudo-anonymous, and how do you allow the sorting, and are there rules and are there moderators? I mean, all these factors. And it's the same thing in games. It has to be. The game manufacturers, in my view, can't deny any responsibility for what's going on because they can affect that.

And even the decision to allow completely open, anybody-can-play-under-any-pseudonym, the sort of maximally free in the sort of libertarian sense environment, that is a decision too. Maybe it's right, maybe it's wrong, but it's absolutely a decision. And once people are getting harassed on your site and racism becomes the norm and threatening women becomes one way or another not just acceptable but a mark of pride, of status, in those places where that happens, to say, "Well, it's none of our business," is just wrong. You set the conditions in which that happens, and so you have at least some responsibility in my opinion and in many people's opinion.

From my point of view, it's exactly the same problem that people who own comments spaces have. They can shut them down because they don't like what's going on with them and it's up to them, but it's not the only recourse. If your comments section has gone wrong, it's because of you. And [with] games, which increasingly are played online, that online interaction is not secondary to the article that was posted but *is* the thing that's being provided. It is the service. Shutting it down is way more consequential obviously for a game company than it is for a newspaper or some other sort of site, but shutting them down is not the only response. There are other things you can try.

VANGIE BEAL, *GameGirlz* founder:
I think there's a history of ignoring. I wouldn't say it's a history of forgiving or forgetting. It's a history of ignoring the issue. You can read the articles online, because these are articles along many of these topics, maybe not quite as search-worthy as Gamergate, but gamers and female gamers being targets of virtual online harassment has existed for as long as I have been playing games online. And I am one of the first females to have ever logged onto the internet and play the game using that technology. [Laughs] People forget. They forget or do they just ignore it? Do they read the articles? They know what's happened, they shrug their shoulders. "Oh, well. Let's move onto the next story."

PAUL GALLOWAY, MoMA NY collection specialist:

It's unfair to single out videogames for misogyny. Come on, look at the art world, look at the film world. A woman, once she gets over forty, her film roles drop off a cliff and you just see a lot less of them. I didn't like [*Inside Amy Schumer*] that much, but there's a great episode where it's your last fuckable day. It's Amy Schumer and Tina Fey and Julia Louis-Dreyfus and they're toasting the day when they're finally too old to be fuckable. They can just let themselves go and be comfortable and don't have to worry about trying to maintain the standard of beauty that's expected of women. It's absolutely the same case in the art world, which is *still* heavily male dominated. Even though museum staffs are primarily women and curatorial staffs at most museums are more women, those women are doing shows about Matisse and Picasso. They're still doing male-dominated exhibitions because that's what people want to see. Maybe in videogames the misogyny is more measurable, because it's written down and you can actually track how many Reddit forums or Twitter threads or whatever baloney you wanted. It's measurable and quantifiable, whereas it's harder to quantify and measure that stuff in art or in cinema.

BEN FRITZ, *Wall Street Journal* bureau chief:

I gave a not-great review on some *Super Mario* game [in 2007 as a staff writer for *Variety*] and people lost their fucking minds and went and sent me these incredibly abusive emails and left incredibly abusive comments on the *Variety* website. First of all, that's never okay. Second of all, I didn't even say the game was terrible. I just said I thought it has flaws, and I was coming from the perspective of not being a hardcore *Super Mario* lover who had played every version of the game. . . . To say the fans didn't take it kindly would be the understatement of the century.

People found *Variety*'s website happened to have an ad for Sony. Like, not the PlayStation. I mean, some other element of Sony happened to be on the website at the same time and there was this crazy theory that Sony had paid me off or paid *Variety* off to run this allegedly negative review of *Mario* and hidden it very poorly. That theory, which got written up on some website, made it to the front page of Reddit.

That was one of the first times I had heard of Reddit. People lost their minds. It's insane, and it just goes to show people, they're so insular and defensive and they want no criticism of *their* games, *their* characters, *their* franchises.

It belongs to them and if, God forbid, anybody comes in with a different opinion, be it someone who's not a hardcore gamer like myself or God forbid be a woman or a person of color or something, they lose their mind. They get really, really abusive and then certain people on the internet encourage each other to do so. And there's nobody out there saying, "No, this isn't okay. I, prominent videogame creator—we, Nintendo, whoever, say this is not okay and we don't want these elements of our fandom and this is not what being a Nintendo fan or a videogame fan is about." Which is absolutely what you see in other parts of the entertainment world.

CHUCK KLOSTERMAN, author/pop-culture essayist:
In my small personal experience . . . it seems as though the insular videogame community has an adversarial relationship with anyone outside of that community having ideas about it at all. [In 2006] I wrote a column about how interesting it was to me that there were no videogame critics who adopted or occupied the social position of . . . The examples I used were [critics] Lester Bangs, Pauline Kael. Interestingly enough, no one noticed—the Pauline Kael mention gets totally dropped. It was just because [*Esquire*] put Lester Bangs in the headlines.

My argument at the time was that it's interesting that this thing that's obviously important is not being discussed outside of this limited sector of society. The response that it seemed to generate from people in the videogame community was that they don't want that. [Laughs] That they're not interested in people who aren't involved with videogames discussing what social meaning that they have. There were also . . . It was a weird thing. By saying that there was no famous videogame critic, it scanned to some people as me saying there are no good videogame critics, and those aren't the same thing. I just thought it was odd that no one has ever crossed over to appeal to people who know of videogames as a meaningful part of society but don't actively participate. And their response was, "Stay the fuck out of it." [Laughs] Like, "It has nothing to do with you."

RAJ PATEL, author/labor activist:

My teenage cousin feels no compunction at all about being sex-ist when he's just completed the odd headshot or several in *Fortnite*. There's no limit to the sexism that spews from his lips. Who in the industry is trying to feel bad about this and how bad are they feeling to the extent that . . . I mean, they're not censoring anyone. They're not setting up norms that seem to matter. So, is this just the videogame industry clutching its pearls but still moving on regardless?

I don't think the creators feel like because they've created this net-work on which hate can thrive, they should be held responsible for the kinds of people they invite on it. And yet there's clearly some relation between the content of what they produce and the biliousness of the comments that get circulated.

It seems to me that there's a dual path forward where . . . absolutely a shaming of people whose racist and sexist and homophobic comments circulate freely on these platforms is important. It's not unusual to have community guidelines. Even Facebook has them, God forbid. And to be able to say, "Look, Facebook, you're shit at community guidelines. This is true. But at least it's hard to find snuff movies on Facebook." There are some things that are pretty easy to legislate and then, yes, there's always going to be a zone of disagreement. To have that end-principle commitment from the videogame-providing network is important. I don't think they've been held to that standard.

It has to be about the players. . . . I think that insofar as change is going to happen, it's going to be driven by the shaming of players rather than the shaming of the architecture of the game or the platform. That has its ups and downs, doesn't it? At the end of the day, legislating for it is much worse than having everyone internalize it by themselves.

ALEX HUTCHINSON, Ubisoft creative director:

I think we made a colossal mistake in bringing the audience in as close as we did. When I was working at Maxis in California, it was the early days of having chats with the community. It seems sort of great and rosy and everyone was saying this is the future of our medium, and I think it's actually become toxic. The fans are not the creators and we don't owe them anything. They have the right to buy it or not buy it. But the idea of engaging with them and giving their voices weight within our studio is something that I find both unhelpful and unhealthy. It's given them a sense of massive entitlement where they feel that George R. R. Martin is going to betray them by potentially dropping dead before he writes the last *Game of Thrones* novel, let alone whether you retuned a rifle in *Call of Duty* and now your family gets death threats. There's this level of negativity that is spawned by letting them speak. I think we should just turn off the valve. We should make our content and listen when we want to listen and not engage as much as we do right now.

There is a potential for it to happen. I think there's a very high possibility. Another way that I like to explain it to people is, at the moment, streamers exist because we give them game content for free, even though basically the act of streaming . . . is illegal. At any point, game companies could turn off the entire act of streaming just by choosing to do so. Allowing it to happen at the moment, allowing them to profit from it, it's like the NFL saying, "You know, we have this thing everyone loves, the football. Let's let everyone broadcast it for free without any restrictions because more people will watch it and then buy tickets to the game." It's inherently crazy. I think at some point, at the very least, EA or Ubisoft or Activision or someone will realize that, "You know, maybe we should just have two really good streamers that'd work for us, that we make money from, and they're the people who are allowed to stream our games. And the rest of these people, these people in basements going around with no oversight and no control valve to make sure whether they're racist or sexist or awful people or what's going on or what the working conditions are like, all this stuff is not healthy for us to engage with."

RICH WEIL, *FusionFall* **community manager:**
I think that what can be done is a little bit of what has been done in fits and starts. But I personally believe if you're gonna be this committed to a cause, if you're gonna be this into it, then there's no need for anonymity. Your employer, your church, your wife, your husband, whoever, they should know that you're doing this. So I think that in the past, if you look at times when people have been actually called out for it, and I mean, I don't necessarily want to use the word "ex-

posed," but where it's been like, "This is a guy who's doing it. It's not AwesomeGamer422. It's Steve Smith. Here's the guy doing this."

I think you have to have accountability for your actions and I think that there's still . . . It's not that they can't be exposed. It's that I think that people are still reluctant to do that. Especially companies are reluctant to do that for legal reasons. I mean, I can only imagine what would happen if they screwed up. You know, you screw up and you say, "Oh, here's David Johnson. He's the guy who's been doing all this horrible stuff." And then David Johnson is like, "Dude, I'm a *priest*. Why are you calling me out? Now I'm getting hammered! I never did any of this. I don't even play computer games." Well, multimillion-dollar lawsuit right there.

CHRIS MANCIL, EA global director of community:

The underground wisdom is 10 percent of the population is insane or crazy, and of that 10 percent, 5 percent may be very troublesome or maybe it's 15 percent. Maybe that's different. The crazy is different than the 5 percent. . . . I think there's just a troll culture—about 5 percent, that makes sense—and there isn't a lot of barriers to them being disruptive. You wanna create online communities that are easy to onboard and easy to be a part of. You don't wanna make being a member of a game community difficult. We spend a tremendous amount of time making it easy to join these communities and then, unfortunately, one of the consequences of that is that it's easy to abuse the rules. And that 5 percent makes a tremendous amount of work for us.

There's a vast, huge silent majority of gamers. People wanna log in and play. They don't care about this stuff. Even the percentage of people who play our games that are interacting with us on social media or log into our online communities is already very small. Most people never engage with us at all. But I would say that of gamers, I would bet the percentage of people who interacted with a bad gamer or troll or bully is unfortunately a pretty high percentage.

DAVID DEWALD, BioWare community manager:

Maybe five per hundred are just there to be an asshole. . . . It's not a lot, but they can be so disruptive and if they've got friends that are being disruptive, too, then three or four people can really feel like ten or twenty if they get on a roll.

FLOURISH KLINK, *Fansplaining* cohost:

Does that mean that the majority of people are fine and it's just a small vocal minority and we should ignore them? Hell no, because the small vocal minority is so powerful in the way that everything is gonna get talked about.

GRACE, *Fat, Ugly, or Slutty?* cofounder:

This is me putting my rose-colored glasses on a little bit, but there's this mathematical thought experiment called the Petrie multiplier. The idea is if you have a particular percentage of people, no matter what gender they are or whatever quality they have, they're going to harass people of the other gender. . . . By the math of it, having 5 percent of your player base who are going to harass women and then having not very many women in your player base, these women will experience *enormous* amounts more of harassment than the average player. Why would we not be striving for a 0 percent rate? My rose-colored glasses are like maybe people think, "Oh, then only 5 percent of messages that an individual person ever sees would be harassment." But, no, the math doesn't work that way.

But it's software, right? That's what always bugged me. You can write something that makes your users not be able to do this to each other.

STEVE JONES, internet researcher/professor:

Should it be anything more than zero? It's an interesting question 'cause I think we're getting to the point where you could address toxicity to that level. It's still Whac-A-Mole, but it's gonna become automated Whac-A-Mole and it's gonna be harder and harder for humans to not get whacked. The degree to which you can automate bouncing people out of a group and not need a human moderator—we're starting to see flashes of this through Twitter and Facebook. I'm sure any game company worth its salt that's got an online game is looking at implementing the exact same thing because that 5 percent, whatever percent it might be, is not going to comprise a sufficiently large source of revenue. In fact, it might prevent other sources of revenue from coming on board such that from a purely economic standpoint, those game companies aren't going to mind losing those players. My guess is that those whatever you want to call them, problem players, are not spending enough on those platforms to matter to the degree that a platform would want to keep them. In effect, if you're one of the first out of the gate with this, you've got a great marketing opportunity to be able to say, "Look, we now have an automated system for keeping people off who abuse whatever policies we've set up. We're a safer place."

HOWARD CHAYKIN, cartoonist:
Zero? And a dream is a wish your heart makes.

DAVID WEINBERGER, *The Cluetrain Manifesto* coauthor:
In the case of games, if I were a game manufacturer and somebody said, "You know, you've done a good job of limiting the amount of toxicity compared to three years ago. So congratulations. But it's still there. I still run into it one way or another. There's still guys calling people who play badly 'fags.' But it's way down, but it's still there." If I were a game manufacturer I would be thinking, and maybe saying, "Hmm, so we could probably limit that by installing some language-recognition software that kicks people off. But that would cost us money, both software and maybe that would introduce lag. I don't know. But also we'd have fewer players. We'd lose all of the homophobic players." And maybe they don't want to make that trade-off. I mean, I'd be happy for them to make that trade-off. But there is some set of trade-offs that keeps them.

It's hard to imagine that there's any game company that likes having racist, homophobic, sexist people exhibiting traits online. Can you imagine? Is there anyone who thinks that's cool or something? I don't think so. If there were, that's a different situation where you just want to shut them down entirely. [Laughs] So they are internally talking about the trade-offs that would be required just to drive it down. Not to make it impossible, because we don't demand that in any of our environments. . . . You can't drive it to zero. You can't drive traffic fatalities to zero, murder rates to zero, or toxic comments in games to zero. It doesn't mean you don't try to get them as low as possible. At some point there is a trade-off. Realizing that there are trade-offs and you're never going to get to the zero does not tell you anything at all about your obligations to try to get it as low as you can.

RICH WEIL, *FusionFall* **community manager:**

There's also another factor, though. You can't look at [toxicity] in a vacuum. You have to look at it with everything else going on. A lot of times I think that the preferred thing to [do is,] like, let's concentrate on the good stuff. Let's get new content out there. Ninety-five percent of our players, they're happy and they're playing the game and they're giving this money and all that kind of stuff. This other 5 percent that's being assholes? [Sighs] We'll do some stuff, but I don't want that to dominate what we're doing for the game. I think that that was part of it and I think that after a while that kind of morphed into: "You're always gonna have the asshole. We're always gonna have 'em. We can't mute everybody so nobody can talk to each other. So what the hell are we supposed to do?"

You're always gonna have those people. We'll put in some safe-guards. We'll put it so you can mute them. Initially, in *Ultima Online*, you couldn't even mute another player. You couldn't block them or anything like that. . . . I think being more willing to put resources into what you can control rather than just throw your hands up—I do think that it would have a positive effect. Some companies are very much that way. Some companies aren't. It really just depends. If there was more uniformity and if there was an acknowledgment of, "Yeah, bad behavior happens in the fringes. Bad behavior happens in the darkness." Then that alone is a condemnation of that behavior. If you know that it's like, "Oh, I gotta go to this special forum to say this crap about this female game developer," well, then you already have to know you're doing something wrong.

SHANNON APPELCLINE, **role-playing-game historian:**

I don't understand. Why do people do this? I don't understand. It's totally alien to me. I mean, I certainly have felt some tribalism within myself, like when someone said they really liked the *GURPS* role-playing game as opposed to the *RuneQuest* role-playing game, I can kind of see it to that extent. I can't imagine telling a *GURPS* role player, "I don't want you to role-play with me 'cause you don't understand what a rune lord is."

I think maybe there's a fear that letting these people in will innately change the community that you love and are a part of. I certainly see that in the comics community when people complain about the diversity of new characters. That's clearly people afraid that the hobby they love is gonna disappear because it's going to be changed. Maybe that's it, but like I said, I don't understand.

AARON BLEYAERT, *Conan* senior digital producer:
Does anybody take the other side? Does anybody defend that kind of terrible behavior?

JENNY HANIVER, *Not in the Kitchen Anymore* founder:
It always seems like it's been an attitude of: "There's only so much we can do." Videogaming is supposed to be fun. People do it to relax, people do it to socialize, whatever. There are a variety of reasons, but overall I believe it's meant to be fun. So if you're running into someone who's following you from lobby to lobby to lobby throwing slurs at you and messaging, that's shitty. It's shitty and it's so lazy for companies not to want to always be working to better the situation and better the community for the players. Why would you want people to think that way about gaming? So many people have just a really negative view of gaming overall.

I don't know what a good solution is. I wish I did. For as long as I've been involved in this, like, I have ideas and *areas* to address, but long-term, until people stop dismissing it as just a part of it and trolling, I don't think it's gonna get fixed. I can't understand why. Okay, so let's say it is just trolling. Let's say that the person saying these things isn't misogynistic, isn't racist, isn't homophobic. *How is this fun?* Like what kind of a person are you that saying this stuff to another human being is fun to you? It just gets exhausting mentally and emotionally because it's so out there. It's impossible for me to understand.

We should be trying harder because a lot of people, they identify as gamers. That's a huge part of their identity and to be dumped into this basket of, "Oh, it's a bunch of teenage boys," or, "It's a bunch of gross guys who live in their basement," why do we have such a negative opinion of gamers? Why are we saying all of these things are negative and just going, "Yeah, it's fine that people view us this way."

CHAPTER 6

THE KIND OF GUY THAT WOMEN WARN EACH OTHER ABOUT

Gamergate and #MeToo

ALBA, videogame streamer:

Just to start from the beginning, I guess, I had just started streaming not even for about a year. I started doing well and picking up speed as a new streamer faster than most people. So, I had wanted to go to Red Bull Battle Grounds [tournament] for the *Starcraft* event they were doing [in 2015]. I managed my stream to help me get the tickets and I decided to go. I went alone. I had never met any streamers in person, I had never seen . . . I had gone to one *Starcraft* event before I even started playing.

But this was my first time going as a streamer, as someone some people there would know who I am, other streamers who knew of me. And it was actually at a venue I'd been to before, The Fillmore Silver Spring. I had gone there for Wolfgang Gartner, who is an EDM DJ, and The Glitch Mob. . . . I knew the venue because it wasn't one of the best venues in the area for that scene. Their security is usually obnoxious. I noted that venue because when you walk in and you have glow sticks on you, anything fun really, they would strip it off you and you weren't allowed to bring it in. Like, no-nonsense place.

And when I had gone to Red Bull Battle Grounds, I remember I was ready: all the stuff out of my pockets. Like, the usual drill. And I remember they looked at my ID and they just waved me inside, didn't even really make eye contact. I thought it was kind of strange from prior experience, but it was a gaming event. Different time of day, different crowd. So I guess everything was a lot more relaxed.

I had been there for about forty minutes. I got myself a Stella. I walked around the venue just to check it out. And then I ran into some streamers I recognized and of course I talked to them. And I'd say, I don't know, forty-five minutes, an hour in? I remember going to the bathroom and then I woke up in a hospital eight hours later completely . . . I've gone out as a person, just, like, my own background: I'm not a shut-in-type person. I spent my early twenties in New York partying a lot.

I've never had any kind of drugging incident happen to me or any-one close to me or anything like that. I guess I would say going to art school in New York in my early twenties there was some recreational activity. I'm not ignorant to the idea of drugs and things like that. I've never been blackout drunk. I know this is in text so: I'm a very small girl, 5'1", 100 pounds. I just can't drink that much. I usually get sick or tired. [Laughs]

It was instantaneous. The last thing I remember was mid-conversation with someone who's an esports translator and host that I knew of. But eight hours later I woke up in the hospital a wreck and I managed to get home. But after that, especially now being a streamer, I was left in shock and embarrassed almost to stream again after that because I didn't know what happened to me over that eight-hour period. But there were comments and stories from people who had been there. A lot of people wrote it off as me just drinking too much, because apparently that's what I did, from what I'm told. [Laughs] I had to see pictures of the event that I'm in on Twitter from other people that I don't remember taking. The whole thing was pretty traumatic.

And the response from the community—well, one, why did this happen? A lot of people immediately would guess a spectator, someone who attended the event, someone who came *for* me. Like, that's what happened. It was a stranger and it was just something that happened. It seemed pretty . . . As I said, people also thought I drank too much. It seemed pretty blasé to people. It wasn't that big of a deal as far as immediate community reaction.

When I walked into that place . . . Like I said I was used to this venue and used to security, and it was actually a complete 180 when

I went for this event, and why is that? Is music more dangerous than gaming? What would be the reason that they personally wouldn't try to at least put a front up of security at these types of events? Are any of these events really taken as a place that could possibly have violence or bad things happen? And I feel because it's gaming, and because a lot of these games are open to people of all ages, it's viewed as almost like a child-friendly community, like, very: it's just a game. You know, games are fun, games are for kids. Malicious adults would not be attending these types of events.

But I feel like those things . . . What makes gaming an industry where those things can't happen either? Why is that level of seriousness not taken with our scene in gaming versus other scenes?

MAUREEN RYAN, *Variety* **TV critic:**

Gamergate was a really bad MRI result that could've been a diagnostic device. And what they decided to do is put that in a drawer and never open that drawer again.

KATE MOSER, Nintendo copyeditor:

The culture that I experienced toward women at Nintendo was extremely toxic in ways that are sometimes hard to put into words. And one of the ways that it was toxic was that it pitted a lot of people against each other for the chance at very few permanent jobs. And when there's a resource gap like that, things get really ugly really fast and especially so for marginalized people. People did things and accused each other of doing things for jobs that would never fly in other industries. . . . I'm not sure I have an answer to why larger studios haven't had any big shake-ups. Part of me wonders if it's because game studios can be an echo chamber for the worst things in society.

An example of this weird culture comes to mind. I have a few friends at ArenaNet and one who left the company about a year ago. One of the things that has put this friend off of gaming is evident in a story she told me about a former writer on the ArenaNet team. This is coming from me through her, which means a couple layers of interpretation, so take it as you will, but here's the story she told me: There was a man on the team who was known for lewd remarks and for generally being a jerk to any woman he worked with. This is the kind of guy that women warn each other about and don't leave their female coworkers alone in a room with. Complaints started happening as soon as he was hired, but nothing was done. When the guy actually assaulted another writer, she came forward to management about it. To their credit, they finally did something about the guy and fired him.

But when they did this, they sent him back into the writers' room to give him the chance to clean out his desk without a security escort. It was during lunch hour, and his accuser was in that same room working alone at her desk with no one else around. The woman got out of the room as soon as she could and found a female coworker to wait with while the guy cleaned out his desk, so the situation didn't turn out the way it could have. But that complete lack of awareness on the part of management speaks to a deep culture of ignorance when it comes to women's experience in gaming culture. It's the "he's probably harmless" and "you're being dramatic" attitude that makes everything that much worse for women in the industry.

LULU LAMER, videogame producer:

Why haven't we taken down major harassers? . . . I kind of suspect that [game companies] *don't need us* the way Hollywood needs women. Hollywood can't survive without women to play the parts. We don't have the leverage in games.

BEN FRITZ, *Wall Street Journal* bureau chief:

I think the problem actually is really bad in Hollywood in particular because it is an industry of gatekeepers and it's not really a career in which you evolve. It's a career in which you make big jumps. So someone like a Harvey Weinstein or a Les Moonves has the power to essentially say yes or no you will get to make a movie, yes or no you will get to star in this film. That is a binary choice with huge implications for someone's career, which unfortunately people are willing to put up with or feel they have to put up with a lot of horrible behavior and abuse in order to get that yes.

Also it's a business in which there are a lot of very subjective decisions about which actress is right for this role, should this movie get made, should this TV show get green-lit? There's no clear yes-or-no answer often. And often, we allowed certain people who will allegedly have great taste or their finger on the pulse of what the public wants to have all that power to make the decision. So they're very, very powerful gatekeepers, and people who really, really want their yes, it profoundly affects their lives. That is a setup for abuse in which an abusive person can really thrive. It has thrived and finally our culture is changing enough that those people are being called out and we're grappling with how to change it.

But it also is true that it doesn't hurt that Harvey Weinstein is famous and he cultivated his fame in many ways to the great benefit of the American indie film business and space. Harvey Weinstein has been a great advocate for it. He's released a lot of films that wouldn't have gotten released otherwise and has made the cinema much better over the past twenty years, but the downside of it was obviously horrific.

The videogame industry doesn't have either. You could argue you could have a Harvey Weinstein–type figure who was advocating for and promoting the indie-games business and indie-game creators, and it's good for games, but the flip side is you might have gotten all the downsides and abuse that come with a Harvey Weinstein. Is the game business probably rife with sexism? Absolutely. Is there anyone who is able to be as abusive as Weinstein or Moonves? Not to my knowledge.

HEATHER CHAPLIN, author/media critic:

Well, are there any women in the industry who aren't in PR and aren't indie-game makers? [Laughs] When I was there, you wouldn't see a woman as far as the eye could see. So I just don't think there are that many women. I'm sure if you dug you would find some sketchy behavior, but my sense is that maybe just there aren't really that many women developers. Are there?

You don't really have Harvey Weinstein or any particular fears of make-or-break all-powerful people like that because it's like if they're make-or-break powerful, yeah, you could lose your job rendering hair. But it's not like if you please the lead designer on whatever the newest game is that you're going to become a movie star and gonna become rich and famous. I'm not sure the same power dynamics are in play.

LULU LAMER, videogame producer:

Games people are spread out, whereas Hollywood is all in one place. We're all locked in our offices in suburbia all over the country and world working long hours. How do we connect and share stories about this shit?

FLOURISH KLINK, *Fansplaining* **cohost:**

Games are more misogynistic than film. *Than film.* [Laughs] I can name so many women of power in the entertainment community and it's really hard to find people in those equivalent positions in games. . . . I think one of the things about #MeToo is that in a lot of the industries that it's come up in, like in the film industry, you have these actresses who eventually can maybe become very powerful who are being preyed upon at a moment in their careers when they're not powerful. You have people who have the potential to become powerful and eventually do. You have also very different gender dynamics in that as an actress you're much more vulnerable to this sort of thing than women in some other roles.

You'll notice that there's not a lot of #MeToo coming from DPs [directors of photography] or people on set. Now, one of the reasons for that is there are so few women in those areas, and when there *are* women in those areas, the kind of harassment is very different. It's more like: "You're not welcome in the boys club." I think that's largely the kind of harassment that people are suffering in games. It's not the same kind of harassment, necessarily, as #MeToo.

If you're being undermined constantly or being told, "You're not a gamer because you're a woman and how can a woman be a gamer?," then that's a different kind of undermining and different kind of misogyny than having your ass slapped and your boobs commented on and Harvey Weinstein wanting to give you a massage. (A), obviously there's different levels of seriousness of these things—I'm not saying there's not—and (B), both those things happen in both places, I'm sure, but I do think that there's a different tenor.

MIKE HILL, videogame/film creative consultant:

I can give you a reason that I believe #MeToo hasn't affected the games industry quite so much: I think it's down to the fact that a large percentage of people that operate in the games industry became competent in their fields because of their specific hesitance to operate in the social field. And that means that in general you get people that can be a bit more sexually dysfunctional, a bit less confident, a bit less aggressive, a bit less socially dominant. Whereas somewhere like the film industry you get a lot of *very* aggressive, ambitious people that are searching for power and prestige, and that comes with it all of the negative aspects that can come with what the #MeToo movement is pushing against. So I actually think that in the games industry, it has a population of people that work in the games industry that are less conventional. They're a very specific demographic and group of people that are less socially dominant, probably less likely to be sexually aggressive.

I mean, that's a very catching statement, but there's a lot of very socially sensitive and socially insecure people in the games industry. When you do hear narratives that are related to the idea of inappropriate behavior in the workplace and whatnot in the games industry, it doesn't have quite the same aggressive flavor as what you hear in, say, the Harvey Weinstein case. I think a large part of it is actually just immaturity on the part of the people in the industry, that they don't know how to behave, as opposed to they know the rules of the game and they're going to break them for power.

You do get guys that have been operating in the games industry that became important in that games industry because they never have had experience in social fields or trying to seduce people. They're introverts that have learned this thing, and then there's suddenly an environment where, as with many environments, they're around other guys that think in similar ways. You can get this very strange bro culture that emerges in games, but it's not a bro culture like in an NFL football team. It's guys that wouldn't know how to survive in a bro culture if they tried.

CLIVE THOMPSON, *Wired* **contributing editor:**

I've written about coders and I've heard some people say, "Well, coders are nerds and so they're not going to be the type of people who would even think to abuse." Like, oh my goodness, that's not the way abuse of power works, right? It frequently even happens subconsciously. It's behaviors that people don't even realize they're doing. Of course nerdy folks can be highly abusive of power, and partly because they don't think of themselves as being powerful. So they will still think of themselves as picked-upon people even when they're in control or when they have power within a particular organization.

HEATHER CHAPLIN, author/media critic:

I know I'm on dangerous ground, but what kind of person goes into the field? I know this is the cliché that everybody wants to escape and that I'll get a ton of hate if I get quoted saying this, but I don't mean "the kind of person" like they're a bad person. I'm just trying to be logical about it. Like, the kind of person who is a hardcore gamer or wants to devote their life to the gaming industry, there are a lot of people who have not had great experience or success with personal relations. I don't know how to say it that doesn't sound like I'm demonizing. I mean, there's a reason we have stereotypes, right?

The stereotype of the geek—and I know the gamers hate this—is of somebody who has been picked on and treated badly and maybe is better at computer things and engineering rather than human relations. Anybody who's ever known a geek, that personality, they've been hurt a lot and rejected a lot and there's a lot of defensiveness and there's a lot of anger. I don't know how to say that. You know, I'm not trying to say like, "Oh, I hate geeks." It's just there is a kind of personality that I think is drawn to this and you just have to be real about that.

JOI ITO, MIT Media Lab director:

Videogames have *always* been ostracized as a recreational thing that made kids stay indoors, had somewhat violent themes, and just were looked at with disdain from most parents. It was always shoved into a subculture. . . . I think the fact that videogames were forced into a subculture caused it to behave that way, and it also caused it to always be in the shadows.

BETHANY MCLEAN, *Fortune* editor at large:

Maybe it's that any industry that has a cult aspect to it gets positioned as something to which the ordinary rules don't apply. Think about Elon Musk and Tesla. People who believe in that company think it transcends basic valuation rules. Maybe it does! Or maybe it's that anytime people see the chance to make outsized returns, they're willing to throw both common sense and ethics out the window. So if a company makes a super-hot videogame, investors are willing to look past the unappealing aspects of it because hey, they might get rich. And if people are making money, they may not want to see the ugly #MeToo aspects of the industry.

MOBY, musician:

My awareness of the enormity of [gaming] came from . . . I forget which *Grand Theft Auto* it was, but I was talking to a friend of mine who's a music-business accountant and the week that *Grand Theft Auto* was released, it generated more revenue than every book, record, and movie released that week combined. *All of them*, combined. The top one hundred albums that week generated one-tenth what that one *Grand Theft Auto* generated. I was like, "Oh my."

LISA NAKAMURA, gender and technology researcher:

For better or worse, the game industry has always compared itself to Hollywood. That's been the benchmark of success, like, "We make more money than Hollywood." They don't have a strong sense of mission really of what they're trying to do, except for make money, which no one respects as a mission.

CLIVE THOMPSON, *Wired* contributing editor:

For all the fact that games have become mainstream, there is still a fence which they don't really register directly on: the great center of the radar for cultural and political critics. You know, the coastal folks who . . . I wouldn't say dominate, because no one really dominates any conversation, but who have a catalytic effect on the conversations that become #MeToo conversations. Those folks, videogames are interesting but not central enough to their culture the way that Hollywood or media or tech is for them to be interested necessarily.

There's plenty there to be reported on, but because it doesn't quite have that star system, because it doesn't quite have that central role in the cultural appetite of the coastal symbolic analysts as it were, that may be another reason gaming has slipped a little under the radar.

ANGELINA BURNETT, *Halt and Catch Fire* **writer:**

These fucking games are being absorbed by millions and millions and millions and millions of people. That's profound. That is not counterculture. That is not outside. That is not a hundred thousand people who travel around the country watching the Grateful Dead. That's Beyoncé. That's a big fuckin' difference.

Maybe it's difficult to accept your place at the center of the culture when places like NPR and the *New York Times* aren't acknowledging your place, but I don't turn to NPR and the *New York Times* to tell me what the culture is doing. They're late. They're behind. They're never on the fucking cusp. I look at other indicators. I look at human beings around me.

ANDRÉS PERTIERRA, r/AskHistorians **moderator:**

If you're outside of a fandom and the only time that X fandom breaks into your world is when you're hearing that someone's getting death threats over something really stupid, it's perfectly understandable to be like, "Holy shit, I should stay the fuck away from that." [Laughs] It's a reasonable human reaction.

EMILY NUSSBAUM, *The New Yorker* **TV critic:**

There just seems like there's something walled off about videogames.

BEN FRITZ, *Wall Street Journal* **bureau chief:**

One thing that was clear to me was the games media was *so* segregated from the rest of the media. You can write about movies and TV and work for a mainstream newspaper or magazine—and people maybe came out of covering different stuff and doing that—but you almost never saw games coverage in mainstream publications. Imagine somebody working at *Game Informer* for five years and then going to work in the arts section of the *LA Times*. I mean, it's crazy, right? You wouldn't. Those two things have nothing to do with each other.

Like, you can work at *Entertainment Weekly* and then go work in the arts section of the *LA Times*. If you cover movies or TV, that wouldn't be a big jump. Not a big deal. People did it all the time, but in games it didn't happen because . . . I mean, to be blunt, games journalists were not real journalists. That was what I found. I was working at *Variety*. I was tasked with covering technology, broadly speaking. I started advocating, "Hey, videogames are part of technology. They're relevant to the entertainment business, and some of the entertainment companies we cover a lot of the time like Disney and Warner Bros. were involved in games. We should be covering this." And they said, "Fine."

I started doing it and then I found . . . I don't put myself out there at the time especially as some amazing hardcore investigative journalist or something, but the basic tenets of journalism that I had learned were not something that I saw being practiced almost anywhere in the game press at all. They just saw their task as feeding information to the fans, and getting a game company to give you some assets first before they gave it to someone else was the peak achievement. There was virtually no reporting happening around the companies. It was only what the companies gave to the journalists. That was it. You go on your previews or go on your junkets and you're basically serving their promotional purposes for them and nothing else.

LAURA MILLER, *Salon* **cofounder/literary critic:**

I'm going to assume harassment and discrimination do happen within game companies, even though it's true that we mostly hear about women being harassed by gamers.

So, my guess would be that there is a lot of overlap and awareness between Hollywood and the news media, and to a lesser degree between core Silicon Valley companies and the news media. As a result, people, particularly people in the media, know who Harvey Weinstein is, and even if they weren't already familiar with Ellen Pao, they know about Kleiner Perkins or, especially, Tinder or Uber.* Sexual-harassment

---

* *Pao v. Kleiner Perkins* was a high-profile 2015 gender discrimination lawsuit filed by Ellen Pao against her former employer, venture capital firm Kleiner Perkins. Pao alleged that she had experienced gender discrimination and retaliation, ultimately losing the case but sparking discussion about gender bias in Silicon Valley. In 2014, Whitney Wolfe, a cofounder of Tinder, filed a lawsuit against the company alleging sexual harassment and discrimination. The case was settled with no admission of wrongdoing, but it drew attention to issues of gender discrimination and workplace culture in the tech industry. Similarly, beginning around 2017, Uber faced multiple lawsuits and controversies related to sexual harassment, discrimination, and workplace culture, leading to the resignation of several top executives and reforms within the company.

scandals about those companies—whose services we use, or who have hired our friends—seem like news to journalists.

My suspicion is that most journalists could not name a major game developer, let alone anyone who ran such a company. Games are really popular and a huge business, but for mysterious reasons they aren't part of "the conversation." They're not on the cultural radar screen of most of my colleagues, and the ones who do play games tend not to think about games and their creators the way they think of films, books, and TV series, as topics of general cultural conversation. And that's partly because a big chunk of those present will have no idea what you're talking about and no interest in it.

BEN FRITZ, *Wall Street Journal* **bureau chief:**

It has historically been rare for mainstream newspapers and magazines to cover videogames even 10 percent as much as they do film or TV, and obviously the enthusiast press is not full of dogged investigative reporters.

I could imagine an article about widespread sexual harassment in the videogame industry getting attention, but there just aren't that many investigative reporters who are interested in or take games seriously, I suspect, so it ends up lower on the priority list compared to other industries that many more people understand like, say, restaurants. Because the videogame industry has never been covered much in the mainstream press as a *business* and because it is rare that coverage focuses on individuals, be they developers or executives, it's hard to imagine an article exposing misconduct by a single person at a videogame studio or publisher getting as much public attention.

CLIVE THOMPSON, *Wired* **contributing editor:**

Software industries enjoy the mystique and mystery behind what they do, such that they like the fact that they can pitch this as being very magical, that they're wizards doing this stuff and no average person could understand it. That's definitely true in the software industry. And so whether that's true in the games industry, I don't know. The paradox of the game industry is that they simultaneously fly beneath the radar and yet my sense from having interacted over the years with videogame makers is that they sort of *wish* they weren't so anonymous. [Laughs] I think they would *like* some of the notoriety that a director has in Hollywood. They can't seem to achieve it! [Laughs]

The industry is maybe simply just of less interest to the part of the mass public that has been responsible for #MeToo. Like, think about it: Where did #MeToo erupt in? Well, it erupted in Hollywood, it erupted in media, and it erupted in tech. And those are all areas where there's enormous interest. I mean, for as much as I say that tech companies have a level of anonymity, there's also a sense of—certainly amongst journalists—there's sort of a sense of disdain and envy for the amount of money that these young people are making. They're sort of grimly fascinated by that area. For whatever reasons, that fascination simply isn't there for the world of gaming.

BRIAN MCCULLOUGH, internet historian:
What's the difference functionally between *Red Dead Redemption* and the next version of iOS or Windows? You have to get a thousand people together on a Bataan Death March to get this product shipped. . . . To me the interesting thing is that I feel like videogames have historical kinship with how comic books are developed. If you know the history of comic books, they came up with their production model based on almost the literal sweatshop model of piecemeal garment-industry work on the Lower East Side in New York, where the artists don't own anything. You're all working together to make the title, [but] the company owns the title and the IP.

Think of it this way: You hear all the time about some software engineer that gets in early at a Google or a Facebook or whatever and ten years later they're worth $100 million or something. There's that "rest and vest" thing, like, once you've created Gmail at Google, you just wait for your options to vest and then you go off into the sunset. Do you ever hear similar stories about that in videogames? I mean, occasionally you do for high-profile rock-star game creators, but you never hear those similar stories about like, "Well, here are the thousand engineers that got rich off of Rockstar." And these are companies that have great performing stocks and are worth tens of billions of dollars, but I don't feel like videogames treat . . . The tech industry treats engineers *as talent*, as someone that needs to be coddled almost. [Laughs] But also another way to say it is respected and treated well and given reward for their work. Whereas I don't get the sense at all that that's how the videogame industry treats its talent.

LULU LAMER, videogame producer:

People are still getting fired for telling their fans who have been harassing and abusing them online for months to fuck off one time. Getting fired? [Sighs] That stuff is horrible and shows that it is still the case that PR is really strictly controlling, but I don't know—the fact that those people actually dared to do it anyway, and to continue having their own authentic voice, that they're even allowed to tweet at all? A guy at 2K Marin very nearly got fired for saying something about some other 2K game, about a Rockstar game on his own private Twitter. It was not *negative*. It was just a discussion point, I believe. It was about *L.A. Noire*. He said the faces were creepy. And, like, it's not super-controversial. [Laughs] Dude nearly got fired. He got a sit-down talking to and, like, "Never tweet about our products again or you will be fired."

ALEX HUTCHINSON, Ubisoft creative director:

Remember that we're still all salaried employees, right? So that's a very big difference to a contract worker or even in the movie business when you're in a production house or in a union basically. So we all work for corporations and corporations have rules of conduct. If you don't want to get fired, then you actually have to abide by the things that you've signed. I think they are getting a little less [stringent] about how hard they control those or how much they police those. So, you can get away with a little bit more and you can be a little bit more of a subjective voice within the organization as long as you don't go too far. But, yeah, we all work for the company. . . . When you see people losing their jobs, it's not the best advertisement for speaking your mind.

CLIVE THOMPSON, *Wired* contributing editor:

Unlike books, but very much like movies and to a certain extent TV, videogames are this very collective art form that require a lot of people. And so there's no single person that's responsible for the whole thing. Very often people have *no idea* who made a videogame. They don't even know the head producer. . . . It's almost more like buying a car where, you know, who was the lead designer for the Chevy Volt? There was one, but you don't know who it is. You just bought the car.

We don't sit around thinking very much about the person who made my laptop and the person who made my air conditioning system or the person that made my car or the person that made my Nespresso machine. They're tools we use. We don't associate with them.

LAURA MILLER, *Salon* cofounder/literary critic:

It's weird the way that journalists have an idea about what is news— interesting to other people—that is based on what is interesting and relevant to them, plus what they feel they have an ethical obligation to be interested in. And that's their reality, which, like most of us, they believe to be an accurate and workably complete version of what's going on in the world.

A big driver of the #MeToo story is that it was about people that the general public felt they "knew," i.e., movie stars. When #MeToo first exploded, some journalists became interested in talking about less glamorous places where sexual harassment occurred, but that interest had a social justice element, so they'd focus on working-class victims or women of color. The game industry fell through the cracks. It was less glamorous than tech behemoths like Facebook and Google but not gritty enough to provide a counterpart to those industries.

And to be honest, I think most non-gamers assume that the people who work in the industry are as "bad" as the gamers of Gamergate themselves. I mean, it's not the gamers who made it so you can shoot a sex worker in *GTA*, right? I'm pretty sure they see most developers as catering to the less savory side of human nature because those are the only games they've ever heard anything about. So I suspect they'd regard ubiquity of harassment in the game industry as too much of a no-brainer to be a story. I'd guess that they assume everyone who works in it is already beyond the pale because pandering to Gamergate types is their job.

I have no idea why the gaming industry attempted no action of its own, beyond the usual reason people ignore this stuff: because it is extremely disruptive to business as usual to call attention to it and demand that there be consequences. People let Weinstein get away with it for years for that reason. The reckoning only came at the instigation of outsiders, and if journalists weren't going to force developers to address it, why would they do it to themselves?

CHAPTER 7

THERE'S A NEW WORST THING ON EARTH THAT HAPPENED TODAY!

Gaming and Extremism

JOE WHITTAKER, counterterrorism researcher:
It's kind of a quintessential *New York Times*–type article that some-one's found something, perhaps a modification of a game or something which isn't particularly pleasant, and then have assumed therefore that anyone who might play that game would immediately start develop-ing (A) bad intentions and (B) potentially start to drive towards bad actions. Now, if you said that about any other single experience and how it might be the sole cause of something, most people would laugh at you. But there are certain things—and I would just lump both vid-eogames and the internet or social media more broadly today when it comes to violent extremism—that we've just developed these very odd moral panics where I don't think the data really supports the kind of conclusions that you see in the media. That they have this kind of—if you want to call it—radicalizing agency within themselves.

The reason why the *New York Times* came to my mind is that within the last year they've had equally lazy titles about how YouTube is this great radicalizer. I'd say a quintessential article in terms of videogames is something along the lines of "the alt-right is recruiting via video-games." They'll have a list of, say, the *Doom* modification that's come back around recently, and then will explain that a lot of alt-righters are playing this game and therefore it's assumed that it's being used for recruitment purposes.

In terms of online recruitment, that's a bit of a misnomer. That notion is not really something that holds. Most of the important conversations are still being had offline. It might be that sometimes you make first contact with someone online, but very quickly that gets taken to the offline domain. So it can be slightly simplistic to talk about online-only recruitment. They instead spend most of their time on end-to-end encrypted apps like Telegram or WhatsApp.

IAN BOGOST, *Atlantic* **writer/videogame developer:**

I'm not sure that these [narratives about gaming and extremists] are that frequently or intensely discussed. I think there was a moment when the idea of internet-driven election interference and the rise of the alt-right was first on the public radar that a number of people observed that community appeared similar in structure and membership to certain kinds of game fandom communities. And that overlapped somewhat with much broader internet pranksters on 4chan and 8chan.* Maybe "pranksters" is even too soft a word for whatever it is they are.

Then we had the memory of the 2014 Gamergate affair, which was essentially an internet smear campaign of a similar kind. So I think there was an initial acknowledgment or curiosity or hypothesis about the connection between those worlds, but I don't know that it was ever proven out continuously—that the connections were deemed to be a historical fact.

MAUREEN RYAN, *Variety* **TV critic:**

I was trying to make people more aware about Gamergate and trying to be one of many people saying, "This isn't just about videogames. This is about something else. This is about using the tools and the tricks

---

* Created in 2013 by Fredrick Brennan, 8chan (later rebranded as 8kun) emerged partly in response to perceived limitations on free speech imposed on 4chan by its founder, Christopher "moot" Poole. Brennan aimed to provide a space where members could have more control by allowing them to create their own boards. While 8chan aimed to foster an even stronger commitment to free expression, its lenient moderation policies have resulted in controversies, and 8chan is associated with the dissemination of extremist ideologies.

and the communities and the communication platforms we thought were gonna save us to not just banish us but make us live in fear."

JASON DEMARCO, Adult Swim senior vice president:

I do think that the average person doesn't know shit about Gamergate and doesn't want to, and I think it's fine for them not to. But we're all online every day, so I think people need to be aware of people who say things in bad faith and make up conspiracy theories about people or things. Clearly that's become a huge and important issue in the last couple years in our government.

VENKATESH RAO, writer/tech consultant:

Yeah, in terms of general commentary, I guess the 4chan crowd is generally viewed as adjacent to the Gamergate gaming crowd, and to the extent that meme culture is a shared overlap region, yeah, I guess there has been a narrative around political influence. I'm skeptical of how meaningful that is. I've been following this stuff for more than a decade now. Some of this stuff starts long before Gamergate, like the alt-right beginning with the NRx* community. There's a whole political subculture there that's kind of vaguely adjacent to gaming in some of the patterns of thought, I would say.

How to put it? There's a very nerdy way of thinking and processing sociology questions that come out of a particular mindset. It launches out in a dozen different directions. That's how you get inceldom, that's how you get otaku culture† in Japan, that's how you get NRx-type political thinking in the US, which, in some ways,

---

* NRx (Neoreaction or Dark Enlightenment) is an online intellectual movement critiquing mainstream democratic and liberal principles. It emerged in the early twenty-first century, expressing skepticism toward modernity and social equality. NRx lacks a unified ideology, and interpretations can vary widely within the movement.
† Otaku culture, originating in Japan, refers to a passionate and dedicated fandom, often associated with anime, manga, and videogames. Otaku enthusiasts, known for their deep knowledge of and enthusiasm for these subcultures, have played a significant role in shaping the global appreciation for Japanese pop culture. The term "otaku" was initially used to describe individuals with obsessive interests, particularly in anime and manga, but has evolved to encompass a broader community united by shared interests in various forms of entertainment. In English, "geek" is closest to the term "otaku."

it looks political, but in other ways it's actually kind of more like comic-book fandom. So there's this thing that started, I would say about ten years ago with a feedback loop between the community's estimation of its own importance and relevance and capabilities, and mainstream culture's acknowledgment and validation of that assumption. It goes in a feedback loop.

In the beginning they saw themselves as extremely powerless, and that's how you get the linkage between, say, gaming, chan culture,* memeing culture, and something like mass shootings. That's kind of where I see the starting point. To me, something like a mass shooting is an expression of a particular pattern of powerlessness. But by the time, I would say, 2012, 2013 started rolling around, I think [4chan] began to sense a little bit of their own power in being able to shape narratives and screw around at low to medium levels of the discourse. And what ended up happening, I suspect—I would put the tipping point somewhere around 2013, 2014—they started getting a true sense of their own power. And by the time the [2016 Donald] Trump election came along, they managed to convince themselves that Pepe the Frog had really influenced the election.

Whether you take it ironically or literally, there's this whole culture of believing that meme culture is actually something mystically more powerful than it actually is, and then that's turning into a self-fulfilling prophecy expressing itself in a virtuous cycle of increasing confidence. And by the time you get to Hillary Clinton saying things like "basket of deplorables," they're trying to view themselves as, "Oh yeah, now we're acknowledged. Now we are mainstream and we can make this happen." And then when events unfold in a particular way, they have the narrative raw material to interpret it as validation of their power.

That's how I see the narrative took root. In that sense I've been tracking it as it formed for about ten years. But in the form that I think

---

* Near-complete member anonymity and minimal moderation. Christopher "moot" Poole, 4chan founder, told the *New York Times* in March 2010: "I get a lot of e-mail messages from people who say thanks for giving them a place to vent, an outlet to say what they can't say in real life with friends and work colleagues—things that they know are wrong, but they still want to say."

mainstream culture first noticed it, I would say the crossover moment was when Hillary said "basket of deplorables" [at a 2016 fundraiser].* That's when it really leveled up 10x. . . . Gamergate was a little bit of a sideshow, but it was close enough to mainstream concerns and happening in parallel with a lot of the social-justice stuff happening in the university campuses and things like that, that it added fuel to the fire.

WAGNER JAMES AU, journalist/Second Life historian:

All these issues are instantiated in one way or another through Trump. That has totally swarmed the conversation. We might not be able to think about it to any great degree until that gets resolved. The folks of Gamergate, they were leveraged by Steve Bannon, who went on to get Trump elected, and he's now pushing white nationalists in Europe. A lot of the Gamergate supporters ended up going to the r/The_Donald and they became Trump's online troll army.

There are active debates whether the actual president of the United States is trolling on Twitter and whether he should be banned from Twitter. We went from literally four years ago debating whether people threatening Zoë Quinn on Twitter should be banned, and now we're debating whether Trump threatening North Korea on Twitter should be banned. So, the conversation has become apocalyptic. [Laughs] I don't know if we have enough attention to focus back on the issues that have sort of metastasized from Gamergate into what we're all dealing with now and has actual world and immediate implications depending on which way it goes.

JASON DEMARCO, Adult Swim senior vice president:

It's ridiculous to say Gamergate is responsible for the way people had behaved during the [2016] election. I think that's an easy scapegoat. It's

---

* During the 2016 US presidential campaign, Hillary Clinton's "basket of deplorables" comment, made at a New York fundraiser, referred to a segment of Donald Trump's supporters she described as "racist, sexist, homophobic, xenophobic, Islamophobic." The remark ignited a mix of responses: while some criticized it for potentially alienating voters and reinforcing perceptions of elitism, others viewed it as a critique of bigotry within Trump's base. Additionally, the phrase was reappropriated and has endured as a badge of honor for supporters.

just another way of saying online assholes ruined games, now online assholes are ruining politics. That's a gross oversimplification.

I do think that it's confusing because it's the same *type* of person, and I'm sure there are a lot of people—especially media people—who the first time they really saw anything like a weaponized group of people attacking someone over something so stupid was Gamergate. I think Gamergate woke a lot of people up, and so they're seeing similar patterns in similar types of people. . . . But that doesn't mean they're the same people and it doesn't even mean that they learned a lesson from those other people.

PAUL GALLOWAY, MoMA NY collection specialist:

It's like you go from videogames to Gamergate to suddenly Trump and all these other guys? [Laughs] Have they really had this much power to change the world? [Laughs] I feel like that's giving *any* art form way too much power. There's clearly already some undercurrents of world malaise that is informing all of this stuff, and we as humans like things to be ordered and understandable. A lot of this stuff, the change going on in the world, we just won't have a handle on until like fifty years from now. We won't know what the various causes were.

But we can't help it. We just are desperate to make order out of chaos, and there's a lot of chaos right now. So what do you do? You re-sort to the easy answers: It's because of immigrants. It's because there's too much soy in our food or it's because guys are playing videogames or it's vaccines or any number of these things. I mean, come on, in the 1950s there were US senators holding hearings about the derogatory effects of rock 'n' roll on the American youth and how it's going to make us fall into the hands of the commies because our young are not out there fighting. They're too busy dancing to this vile music by Elvis Presley shaking his hips all sexy.

Humans have always wanted the easy answer to something, and there's a lot of very vexing, extremely hard-to-get-your-head-around kinds of problems going on right now. It's just gonna continue to default to these simple answers, many of which are lazy. They're lazy. Oh, just blame the Mexicans, blame the gays, blame the GOP. It's always more complicated than any of those simple answers.

JOE WHITTAKER, counterterrorism researcher:

I think we're just repeating history. In the '90s, when first-person shooter [videogames] were becoming more popular, there was this often-theorized link between playing these sorts of games and engaging in violence themselves. Again, the data never really supported it.

The thing that I think is quite interesting is the thing that is demonized is very often a part of youth subculture. So it is something that the young people of that day are playing or doing or engaging in that the power holders, i.e., the generations above them, do not understand. And it is something very often that is very new to them. So they don't necessarily . . . It is, again, very easy to find that thing, ascribing blame for something that you don't understand very well.

AARON BLEYAERT, *Conan* senior digital producer:

I mean, you remember Metallica devil messages in the music in the '80s? I think every form of entertainment has gone through something like this before it got adopted by the mainstream, fully embraced by the mainstream.

GINA HARA, filmmaker:

"Don't watch too much TV or you're going to become a serial killer."

RAWN SHAH, *Playing MUDs on the Internet* coauthor:

People blamed MUDs for dropping out of college a lot. [Laughs] Is that a societal problem?

RICHARD BARTLE, online game pioneer/researcher:

Before videogames, what would it have been? It would have been videos or something like that. Before videos it would have been the movies, before movies it would've been television, before television it would've been the radio, before the radio it would've been vaudeville. Before then it would probably have been penny dreadfuls or something. I mean, you go back, people used to complain about the *waltz*. It's people who don't understand things complaining about things that they don't know.

DAVID CROATTO, *MAD* magazine senior editor:

I'm sure you can find a fucking op-ed piece from 1897 blaming the hoop and stick for teen crime or something. [Laughs] Anything that's popular or faddish, there's someone who's like, "Well, we didn't have this when I was a kid and we weren't doing that." But yeah, the world keeps getting more complicated.

I haven't followed the videogame, that scapegoating. But what it has in common, I think? Anytime there's something that people don't understand—whether it's communism or homosexuality or school shootings—the impulse is to blame it on something else that they don't understand. So it's like, "Oh well, you know, comics, they turn kids into murderers." *Seduction of the Innocent** was . . . Every social ill [was] because of comic books. And it was the same with rap music. It was the same with videogames. It was the same with fucking $100 sneakers [that] were the reason that people were killing each other.

CHUCK KLOSTERMAN, author/pop-culture essayist:

The reason people didn't want their kids reading comic books is because they were perceived as frivolous. You'd want your kid reading *Little House in the Big Woods*. You wouldn't want them looking at a Spider-Man comic book. Now comic-book movies are the dominant form of film. Has that been good for the culture of film? I'd say probably not. I would say that film culture now is a little more frivolous than it was in the past.

There seems to be a history in writing about popular culture where the criticism of some new concept is mocked and laughed at. And then time passes and in retrospect, it seems like the criticism was completely accurate. For example, when MTV came out in 1981 and all of a sudden television was, instead of being in half-hour, hour blocks, it was in these little four-minute blocks. Everyone said, "This is going

---

* Published in 1954 by psychiatrist Fredric Wertham, *Seduction of the Innocent* argued that comic books were responsible for juvenile delinquency and moral decay, prompting congressional hearings and the establishment of the Comics Code Authority, a self-regulatory body imposing strict censorship guidelines. Despite widespread concern at the time, Wertham's claims have since been criticized for their lack of scientific evidence.

to destroy kids' attention spans. They're not going to have any kind of attention span anymore because of MTV." The sophisticated view at the time was, "That's ridiculous. This is just part of change. It's an evolution in entertainment. This is different." I'm sure people said that about novels in the '20s. But now looking back, it's pretty obvious that attention spans have decreased in people. Not just in kids, but in adults.

It seems as though all of the things they said that the 1980s were gonna do to people have happened. So, a lot of the things with gaming, the things people are suggesting that gaming is doing seems kind of ridiculous in the present tense. But I do wonder if in twenty-five years, at least in broad strokes, if the things people are concerned about videogames will come to fruition, if they will seem true. . . . I think videogames are great, but they're not *completely* great. [Laughs]

ROGER SHARPE, pinball designer:

Footloose was based on a real story. Children weren't allowed to go to a dance, or there had to be space in between the boy and the girl when they were slow dancing because God forbid their bodies should touch. I just think that there is a sense of responsibility that we have tended to give up, societally.

The research I did for my pinball book about forty-plus years ago revealed this deep-seated fear that pinball machines were evil, that they were games that were stealing children's lunch money, that the mob was controlling pinball machines, because of course the mob needed to generate lots of pennies, nickels, and dimes to support whatever illicit activities that they were doing. And you realize how ludicrous it all is.

LINDA CARLSON, Sony Online Entertainment community manager:

Humanity itself hasn't changed very much in the last five hundred thousand years. We're still treating each other badly, we're still killing each other, we're still grabbing each other's stuff—obviously there's not much you can do about scarcity of resources until we all agree to share. The second thing is that we are all intimidated, frightened, and therefore hateful of groups that we do not understand.

This is just how our species is wired. We are hard-wired to protect our own interests, to be selfish. I mean obviously we try to be unselfish, but as a species we're selfish. We fear others, we loathe others. And that's just the way we're wired genetically. It's going to take a lot of growing up in order to get past that. And we're not there yet.

HOWARD CHAYKIN, cartoonist:

[Sighs] Every generation knows the media lies about it in every way, shape, and form and yet at the same time takes as gospel what that same media says about other generations either before or after them. And I have to take with a grain of salt everything that's being said in print and in media about the millennial generation, about iGen [aka Gen Z] as well, because they lied about mine so completely and consistently and have since I was old enough to be lied about. I have to assume that that same media is fucking up and lying about them as well.

DAVID CROATTO, *MAD* magazine senior editor:

I would say definitely we're bigger idiots than we used to be, we're more gullible. [Laughs] Look, we question whether the Earth is round. We question whether vaccines are a good thing. We question every-thing. You know, stuff that was taken for granted. Like, no, that's a good thing. That's been scientifically proven for hundreds of years.

I mean, I think this is directly linked to the internet. There's all of this shitty, crazy echo chambers where people can get themselves riled up and just bounce this misinformation back and forth. Whether it's that or it's that Obama's a Kenyan. In general, we're stupider. But there's also that the fact-checking of our society has become so de-mocratized that it's dangerous.

JOE WHITTAKER, counterterrorism researcher:

Human beings are quite hard-wired to understand single-narrative explanations to something. Whatever it is, we are at our highest level of ease if we can explain something bad that is happening with one cause and one effect. Clearly, when you think about it for more than a minute, you understand that these kinds of problems are really, really complicated and really, really nuanced. But it is much, much easier, considering if we had to apply that level of nuance to literally everything that we encountered from day to day, we would just end up exhausting ourselves. So it makes a lot of sense for our brains just to accept some things.

In a lot of ways in which the media reports, and I think that can be linked to politics in other ways as well, people are very, very attuned to understanding a single conception of an explanation. And something like "videogames are bad" or "YouTube is bad" stops us from having to concentrate on the fact that there are a very, very large number of reasons as to how we are in the situation we're in. Probably so many that the human brain couldn't even really comprehend them. So instead of doing what we should do, of saying try not to throw the baby out with the bathwater, we end up just blaming one cause.

IAN BOGOST, *Atlantic* **writer/videogame developer:**
The broader culture utterly forgets about videogames every two years and they have to be reminded that they exist. And often that reminder comes in the form of "and they are bad." And so the failure of games to become a mainstream media form in the fifty years of their commercial life is an interesting phenomenon partly to blame here. And so because of that, games still feel scary or unfamiliar or weird or prurient or kind of lower than low culture to different groups. Some say that they're being scapegoated, but that's maybe too simple an explanation. It's more that they're unknown and the unknown is scary, and so connecting the unknown to a threat or an undesirable consequence is an easy way to explain it.

And I don't mean that in a conspiratorial way, like there's some sort of anti-gaming guild or something out there seeking to connect games with negative political outcomes. There are some of those kinds of folks, and suddenly it's the same sort of move that certain kinds of political positions would take with respect to immigration and anything else, gun control. But in the case of games, there really is a kind of deep and repeating ignorance, and that makes it much easier to make those kinds of skin-deep claims. It also is this oil-and-water kind of process where games somehow get separated out from the rest of the media ecosystem.

In fact, if anything, the alt-right as it mainstreamed became its own subjects, and you didn't need the game part anymore. There's a cynical view of this. This is an extremely cynical view, which is that the community of game players or game-adjacent critics were eager to have some kind of importance and even superordinate role in whatever the calamity was that took place between 2014 and 2016. And there was even some pride in having kind of been there first, even if no one did anything about it or even if they couldn't. I think it connects to a kind of broader anxiety and bitterness in game culture, including those who are deeply critical of it, to be acknowledged and not to express the idea that they have been somehow slighted or overlooked.

SOREN JOHNSON, *Civilization IV* **lead designer:**
There's this general sense that game communities are very insular, like they don't have any other outside influences. I don't really think that's true, but I do think that game communities are one of the first net-native community groups. That's their default state. Occasionally things can happen like in real life, where people could meet, but generally speaking, you're using the same machine. You're talking about the thing that you do it on, the same machine that you do it on. Everything fits together. So it just means it's very easy to access all those people in one place, as opposed to "right-wing group tries to convert football fans." Logistically, what does that even mean? [Laughs]

LORA KOLODNY, CNBC.com tech reporter:
This is a social media thing. I don't know that it's gaming. I mean, the games do engender . . . You get that feeling. [Laughs] When you've been playing a first-person shooter for a while, you get the feeling of walking out the door and kind of seeing things as if you were still in the game.
But I get that with other software. I remember having this feeling when I first started working primarily on Windows or whatever it was from some early, early job I had and I'm spending way more time on computers than I ever had before. And it wasn't just word processing. . . . I remember when I was using email and FTP and shared file folders on a network and things like that, I, in my mind, getting out of work as I would be relaxing and shifting from work to a non-work mode mentally, I would sometimes see in my mind that stupid Microsoft icon of files going into the garbage can or leaving the garbage can. I remember it literally just being emptied, the trash being emptied in that stupid Microsoft animation. So I'm not saying games are the only thing that can do that. TV can do this. I am guessing magazines had an

outsized influence back in the day, magazine advertising. In general, pop culture has this effect.

And on the one hand, I don't think the gaming industry itself has provided the right tools to ensure the safety of children or vulnerable populations. This is something all the social platforms are dealing with. Gaming didn't realize it was going to turn into a social network. Game makers didn't realize their games were going to be a room where you hang out, a public square.

STEVE JONES, internet researcher/professor:

Videogames? I mean, I think it's really overstating whatever influence they have to put any degree of primary causality on them. For a couple of reasons. One is that there are positive outcomes from gaming that people tend to overlook too. Obviously there's a social component that I think is worthy of consideration. There's a learning component. There was a period of about ten years when my students would tell you that their single favorite game, and the one that taught them a lot, was *Oregon Trail*. I don't think that game scarred them, right? I mean, I don't think it had horribly deleterious effects. So obviously, there are takeaways, if you will, from different games. It's sort of like saying, "Well, everybody reacts the same way to an episode of X TV show or Y movie." So that in and of itself augurs some caution when it comes to generalizing about videogames.

The other reason is nobody yet, despite decades of effort, has found a way to cause people to interpret and/or act on media messages exactly the way that a creator wants them to either deliberately or on accident. So you could say, "Well, okay, you know, the creators of *Minecraft* or *Clash of Clans* or whatever mass game is out there didn't set out to ruin kids' lives or to cause them to not study and become dumber or something. They didn't set out to do that. Well, they did it, but it happened by accident." Really? To how many people? It's science fiction: you've *unleashed* the virus that's turning everybody into a zombie.

There's absolutely no empirical evidence that this is even possible, and people have taken kids and adults into labs in controlled settings. [Laughs] "Play this, play that." We do this with violent movies or TV shows, with violent music videos. We've done this with all sorts of stuff and you find that as often as not people become desensitized to violence or they come to abhor it, they become less likely to be violent, they become more likely. We are for better and worse, and I'd like to think for better, not controllable to that degree.

LORA KOLODNY, CNBC.com tech reporter:

Kids are smarter than we think. People, gamers, are probably way smarter than you think. Social media users are way smarter than we think. Readers of news are way smarter than we think and they tend to get hip to it. But some portion of them will not be able to overcome negative effects. And so, you gotta be worried about the vulnerable population, the minority of people that will take it too seriously and feel suicidal or who will fall prey to a white supremacist group.

I have a friend who when we were kids, his parents were divorced . . . [He] was *pretty much* on his own at like age fourteen, fifteen and got targeted and swept up by a white supremacist militia in our town. And I saw firsthand what he went through.

I was scared of him when he was part of that but still tried to occasionally talk to him and hoped he would come back around to reason and be a regular human. It took him years and it ruined his life, and he became severely drug- and alcohol-addicted and lost all his teeth pretty young. There are still effects on his life today. He's all right, but this happens to not-gamers, is what I'm saying. He was a skater. He wasn't a videogame kid. We were into punk rock and skateboarding. This was before interwebs were a daily part of our lives.

I'm not trying to say this is only a gamer thing, but I am trying to say those platforms have introduced unique challenges. When you're bringing a group together online and you allow strangers to infiltrate that social group through these chat apps and things that you've designed to be "fun" or "increase engagement" or bring gamers back daily . . . you need to be cognizant, you need to be transparent, you need to be open to third-party research, you need to let the psychologists understand it and not just so you can exploit it. You *need* to take responsibility.

Those who are being radicalized . . . What about those who are being psychologically abused and are building up an immunity to getting trashed? To being demeaned? To seeing their peers demeaned? You don't think that impedes bonding? You're going to have people with attachment disorders or generalized anxiety. . . . Everyone needs to take a good, hard look. You don't know what the kids are dealing with. A majority might be safe, but why don't these companies care about the minority that aren't?

IAN BOGOST, *Atlantic* writer/videogame developer:

Think of the games industry as all of the worst aspects of Hollywood plus all of the worst aspects of Silicon Valley. That's sort of the summary. They don't necessarily always carry out that nastygram in practice, but that's the default attitude. So what that means is, you've got a group of people who are mostly driven by just worker bees trying to make a living under extreme conditions where they're actually treated worse than filmmakers because they're not unionized, because they're employees rather than being independent contractors moving from project to project. Then, in the case of the folks who would be creative executives in another kind of medium, they're just business-people there. They're running studios or they're operating the market segmentations in order to determine which version of a franchise to develop, like studio executives.

On the Silicon Valley side there's this sort of strong libertarian bent—which I think the games industry broadly speaking very much shares—which is one of the causes of the lackadaisy that we see in those companies today, Google, Facebook, and so on, like, "Well, you know, it's not really our problem to figure out how to police speech online. We can't do it even if we wanted to because there's too much content. People should be able to say whatever they want anyway." Any of the number of different kinds of positions that you see on that matter.

HEATHER CHAPLIN, author/media critic:

You could take two positions. One, you can say, "Well, it's unintended consequences, which almost by definition can't be foreseen." Or you can say, "Are you fucking kidding me? You couldn't have foreseen this?" This isn't game-specific, but I think that we are living in a time where we worship innovation for innovation's sake, and the Mark Zuckerbergs of the world, they remind me of little boys just pulling the wings off butterflies.

It's no ability to think holistically or systemically. I get it, like, in his dorm room, Mark Zuckerberg could not have known that Facebook would become this unbelievably society-altering thing, but at some point along the way they did start to think that, and to think that you could drop something like that in this society without ripple effects seems to me just myopic to the point of being criminal negligence. I've thought about this a lot in terms of social media companies.

I mean, I was incredibly struck in the mainstream game industry by how apolitical it was, that people really wanted to be seen as creative actors and artists. But they had *none* of the characteristics I'd seen in every other artist or creative community, which is an interest in the world, a curiosity about the world, and caring about the state of the world and the effects of their art on the world.

BRENDA LAUREL, Purple Moon cofounder:
If you're talking about the game industry now, when they say, "Do hard things," they're talking about graphics and animation. That's their notion of hard. It's the iceberg that you don't see the tip of, this business of, "Oh wait, who is this for? How is this going to affect their lives? Who are these people and what might they like? What might make them happy?" The industry has never asked those questions in any consistent or deep kind of way because it's invisible to them. The players are marks, they're customers, they're statistics. They're not people. It's not in the DNA of the game industry to think that way.

LORA KOLODNY, CNBC.com tech reporter:
I don't think less of the kids that get pulled into that any more than I would feel . . . I'm not happy about it, but I look on these kids that are enticed into negative or extremist groups and conduct online the same way I do with gangster militias offline or social media use. Like, you have these pro-anorexia communities on Instagram that darkly exchange tips and tricks about how to be sicker and sicker. To me, it's just another . . . For any platform to assume the extremism won't be there, the predators won't be there is really naïve. It's neglectful, it's problematic. But I don't personally blame the game players. I think they have been misled, enticed.

I think so much of this is informed by a wish [for game companies] to position themselves like the social media platforms have, as a company that doesn't have any liability or responsibility or legal burden to address this. If they begin to acknowledge it, it opens a floodgate for lawsuits. There's a law that allows social media platforms in the US not to be responsible for the content posted by users. That law allows tech companies to basically shrug and go, "Our users did it." Meanwhile, the users are like, "*You* gave us the tools. I was just doing what I thought I was allowed to do based on social norms." You know, everyone's pointing the finger. Nobody wants that liability.

JOE WHITTAKER, counterterrorism researcher:

I would link it back more to social media companies. We do work with them quite a lot and do engage in a productive dialogue. Certainly not all of them, but most of the big players, even though they recognize that there are really, really difficult problems on their platforms, are willing to engage in research and listen to our findings when we talk about them. So I would say it's probably not a good sign if the game industries are just not even willing to engage in any kind of dialogue. But at the same time, it doesn't seem reasonable to me to assume guilt just because they aren't necessarily as cooperative as researchers would like.

This is pure conjecture, but yeah, if the comparison is against social media companies, it seems that [game companies] are less willing to talk about problematic elements on their platforms than social media companies. Now that might of course be a result of the fact that over the last ten years, governments have bloody well forced social media companies to engage in a dialogue because this really widespread problem was realized on their platforms. If the same thing had happened on videogame platforms, it might be that they would also have been forced to.

IAN BOGOST, *Atlantic* writer/videogame developer:

The games community, for whatever reason, is unable to believe that they are not this big important thing that is undeserving of the ill treatments that they sometimes receive. I think it's just very, very, very hard even for very smart, attentive people inside of the industry or the community to get that they're still a quite marginal domain. I don't know how to solve that, but I think that until there's that recognition—which I had a number of years back with my own work and have been trying ever since to work through and still haven't really found a synthetic approach to—that there's a reason why when [the popularity of] *Fortnite* happens, everybody freaks out and then there's articles that are like, "What the hell is *Fortnite?*"

It's because it's incomprehensible to a large segment of the population that isn't naturally against it but also is deeply unaware and concerned about their unawareness. Every now and then I fall into one of these—because they're still running in the community—disputes or whatever, and they're just *so small-scale*. This week there was something about game difficulty? I guess this was the flare-up of the week. In part it's like unless you're paying attention all the time to the whole of the community, you don't even really know what the issue is. You have to sort of dredge off where it's sourced from. But just seeing those articles and comments and tweets and whatever, interspersed with all of the rest of the stuff that I look at, it's just very clear that the perspective on the matter is for many in the game community quite, quite deeply skewed.

It's not that it's not interesting or an important problem even. I don't know if it is or it isn't. The way that that comes off and how it looks, the texture of it and the amount of prior knowledge and the depth of attention and concern and experience you have to have even to know what is going on, even to know what anyone is talking about, it's so wonky. That's just very hard to rise above and kind of go, "Okay, okay, okay, what's really happening here? What are we talking about? Why does this matter? Why would it matter to someone to whom it doesn't already matter?" Unless that sort of situation is alleviated or dissolves itself, then I think we'll just keep seeing these cycles of ignorance and decay and then more ignorance and more decay over time.

The thing about wonky communities is that . . . You know when you're talking to someone and they sort of pause and they go, "Okay, like, this is super inside baseball. This is really wonky. Maybe you don't wanna hear about this."—there's a sort of recognition that, okay, I'm now diving into the private knowledge of an expert domain and stop me if it gets confusing and we'll come back out again and see if we can try. That doesn't happen with games. There's not a lot of mainstream venues for it. It sucks in that way when you write about games for a general reader and do that work. You always get sneered at: "Oh, look at them, trying to explain what a deathmatch is." Well, it's because it has to be explained, actually, and I'm sorry that it bothered you.

So I think this is a tension and a playing out of that tension between that safe space, private community, where there's something that is yours as a gamer that others don't have access to and the simultaneous desire for it to be everywhere and for it to be important and influential. And they're fundamentally at odds, and I don't think that the practitioners in the space necessarily see it that way 'cause they want both. They want it to remain private and secluded, but also they want it to be universal and important.

JASON MANNING, author/sociologist:

I think [people making links between extremists and gaming] might have something to do with just the fact that subcultures or people who are unconventional often seem to attract more liability for things or to be somehow scarier. It's an identifiable group and they're weirdos, that kind of thing.

Why people don't recognize they're repeating is probably most people just don't know much of history or even what happened last month. Things seem to fade from public consciousness quickly. [Laughs] It's like a cat playing with tinfoil or something. "This is the worst thing on earth to happen today!" And then two weeks later it's forgotten about. "There's a new worst thing on earth that happened today!"

RUKMINI PANDE, race and fandom researcher:

Partly the eagerness to write about and to be *right* about it is motivated by the fact that in this economy, the way that journalism and writing about culture is going, the more you produce and the faster you produce it, the greater your ability to make a livelihood out of it is. And I'm part of that. I'm not trying to say I'm not. If I haven't reacted to whatever's happening in fandom, I feel like I'm missing out. I feel like I haven't made enough of an impact.

That point of view leads to bad scholarship because it leads to ahistorical thinking. So everything is new and everything is right now and everything is the cause of whatever crisis that is happening, and people seem to get enough of the dots in place and then want to diagnose it. . . . I see some of my US friends who I've had conversations with about the problems with political culture historically, and all of these people do know that all the issues with American politics did not arise in the last year. [Laughs] But they seem to be forced into positions where there is not much room for nuance.

I think that's also a problem because you're not just talking about Gamergate. You're talking about the position of identity politics in the US today. You're talking about what does being American mean? And somehow videogames become . . . Not to downplay their role or how they reflect various aspects of US identity, but this is a very global transnational community. So that does frustrate me because we're never talking about any other aspects of these communities. And they're very flexible, they're very mobile, and it's really difficult to be like, this is what gaming culture is. And yet that's what we get again and again.

India is not much better. It seems to be a problem worldwide, where you're being pushed into positions where you're on a side and you have to dig in and not allow for nuance for those kinds of discussions. And that's bad. I do identify myself as somebody who holds left of center views, and I can see people making ahistorical comments and analysis because we just need to be right and we need to make an impact because the stakes seem so high.

JOANNE MCNEIL, art critic/writer:

The media is reactive rather than proactive. . . . I remember thinking that while Gamergate was happening, "How many spaces were complaining instead about trigger warnings and college-campus protests?" This is something I was just thinking the other day because there was that *Slate* piece about the Yale Law School inquiry about Jed Rubenfeld's harassment of students. And I remember reading it and thinking, "A lot of the people I know that are public intellectual types, just four years ago they would have been complaining about student protests on Yale as if the students were to blame." When, here's an example of someone that really ratcheted up that hostility towards students who was apparently harassing students.

These kinds of things, they come to light now, but we'd be in a better position if people back then had given a little bit more time to people who were powerless or with significantly less power than the people that were castigating them just in general. I think a lot of those dynamics were happening at the same time as Gamergate and maybe a few people have, you know, come to grips with the reality of racism, sexism, transphobia, and other kinds of hatred toward a less privileged people.

But we would be in much better shape if they had realized this early, which to me says, What are we ignoring right now? What kind of issues are people ignoring at this moment? Would that be climate change? Would that be class issues? The nature of the job reports look good, but why are most jobs at Amazon factories? These circumstances that would be better if people were aware of them now so we don't screw up later on.

VENKATESH RAO, writer/tech consultant:

Ignore the post-truth or fake-news spin. This is more like a regime of unfalsifiable ambiguity and chaos, where certain people have a need to hold simple mental models of complex things go looking for whatever will clear that simplicity. . . . You want a simple world. You want a world with cardboard cut-out villains. You want a big conspiracy theory where there's really just a bumbling huge government apparatus.

Essentially what we have is things are complicated, messy, and noisy, and that's just the way it is. Software is eating the world. Lots of things are changing. So there is a lot of messiness, and a certain kind of person who cannot handle the basic increasing messiness level, they make up these self-satisfying stories. . . . This is not really a truth process. This is more sort of a reality-construction process where you're trying to create a reality, a game-like reality. There's a sort of rhyming with the gaming world more than a literal connection.

So you've got to be careful about . . . the direct impact of anything, whether it's comic books or people staring at phone screens too much. It's useful to come at it from [different] directions. One is the actual macro-level numbers of statistics. If you actually try and count the young incel white gamers who have just exited college and can't find jobs and are living in their parents' basement supposedly playing videogames all day because that's more fulfilling for them than actually working a minimum[-wage] job . . . they don't have enough numbers to actually swing anything. That's literally true. I would say not only do they not have enough raw numbers to swing anything. They literally probably don't even vote. The narrative is statistically wrong.

But, having said that, you cannot underestimate the importance of small forces really steering narratives in leveraged ways. You can think of it as some small inciting event where maybe some left-wing commentator says something and then some right-wing trolls blow it up out of proportion. Then somebody at the *New York Times* decides to turn it into a story and one data point becomes a mass demographic trend in the head of a *New Yorker* writer and then that blows up. . . . I think the perception of gamers by the mainstream is now such a caricature you can basically ignore it.

CHAPTER 8

TROLL CULTURE

*A Thing That Happened
Because People Liked Lookin'
at Pictures of Cats with
Funny Phrases on Them*

STEVE JONES, internet researcher/professor:

One of my mentors from years ago, he had this wonderful phrase that Americans are forever trying to build the city on the hill and then trying to get out of town. We build these ideal communities and then we hate 'em and we leave 'cause we can never do the ideal. I mean, there's always gonna be some flaw. There's always gonna be some issue and we're gonna wanna get out of town.

This is not a technologically induced failure. People have been assholes a long time before we had the internet or really any form of computer-mediated communication. The scale of the . . . I don't have a good word for it. "Assholedness" is not a word. It was much harder to be a jerk at the scale and at the speed with which one can now be given any computer network, particularly the internet, but then that's true for . . . I mean the internet's amplified everything. . . . Certainly The WELL,*

---

* Founded in 1985, The WELL (Whole Earth 'Lectronic Link) is one of the oldest virtual communities. Katie Hafner's 2001 book *The Well: A Story of Love, Death & Real Life in the Seminal Online Community* describes members as ranging from "technologists to business people to Deadheads" who shared "electronic postings [that were] as revealing as diary entries."

certainly PLATO,* certainly Usenet,† certainly bulletin-board systems all had it.

REVA BASCH, Women on The WELL conference host:

I think it would be a huge fallacy to extrapolate from The WELL because it was so civilized. Insular, in a way. It had rules people pretty much abided by even at the same time as they were making fun of them. The rest of the internet, Usenet, and so on, everything else that was happening out there—okay, there were other BBSes‡ and some of them were very much geared toward nerds and with a whole craziness of Usenet as you drilled into it. But The WELL was *not* representative of any of those other areas. It really was its own thing.

I mean, I hate to use an extreme metaphor like, I don't know, a convent or a monastery or something like that, but we really were in a way sequestered from the rest of the net and took a certain pride in that. At the same time we realized that, yeah, maybe we weren't represented in the real world. When you seed a place with journalists and Deadheads by giving them free accounts, I don't think you're going to have a population that's typical of the rest of the world. So, huge fallacy to extrapolate from The WELL, although The WELL had its own issues, certainly.

There was one particular episode that I think is emblematic of The WELL as a culture and Women on The WELL as a strong community,

---

* PLATO (Programmed Logic for Automatic Teaching Operations) was designed for computer-based education in the 1960s, and in 1973 the system expanded its capabilities to become one of the world's first online message boards. Brian Dear's 2017 book *The Friendly Orange Glow: The Untold Story of the PLATO System and the Dawn of Cyberculture* describes the system as the "first online community."

† A precursor to contemporary online forums, Usenet—established in 1980—was described in Ed Krol's 1992 "complete introduction to the internet" compendium *The Whole Internet User's Guide & Catalog* as an "informal, rather anarchic, group of systems . . . similar to 'bulletin boards' on other networks. USENET actually predates the Internet." In December 2023, Google announced that Google Groups would end support for posting or viewing new Usenet posts in February 2024.

‡ Popular in the pre–World Wide Web era during the 1980s and early '90s, bulletin-board systems were local computer systems that allowed people to connect via modems to exchange messages.

and that was the cybercad scandal. That happened in, I believe, '93. *Time* magazine covered it, the *Washington Post*, *New York Times*, *Chicago Tribune*. Mr. X or the cybercad, basically he came on to a number of women—he was a WELL user—and one of whom, he was telling her, promising her . . . I think she might've even loaned him money or something, and then radio silence. She came into Women on the WELL and said something about this guy.

And another woman said, "Wait a minute, that sounds *really* familiar." And it turns out that there were four or five women who were in the women's conference who this guy was either coming onto or with whom they had actually hooked up and he had borrowed money and this and that. And it just seemed like: "Oh, you know, this is not right." And we talked about what to do, and given the norms of The WELL, it was just this guy was being really shitty. The sense of the women's conference was that the host, i.e., *I*, would start a topic in a public conference.

The news conference was sort of the main central square or whatever of the village known as The WELL. Everyone stopped by the news conference to see what was happening. And I started a topic—I think it was topic number 1290—about this guy and I forget what I called it, but it just started this firestorm of reaction. Some people were going, "Well, what the hell, you're grown women. Deal with it." But I think the general sense was of outrage because he wasn't acting right action in that kind of almost samurai sense that was a big part of The WELL mores, and this guy was just a douche. People were going, "Okay, get over it! This is a witch hunt." The word "witch hunt" was used.

I think the guy eventually left The WELL, but I don't believe he was barred. I'm a little vague on what actually happened. . . . But the reason why it just remains as a kind of core memory of the period when I was hosting was that he violated community standards. He was just not a good person, not an honorable person in that respect. I don't think you'd call it harassment. I don't think it would fit into that category. There were other incidents in the public WELL where some much more serious personal harassment—if you want to call it that—went on. But within Women on the WELL, not so much. That was the one case that really sticks in my mind.

BRIAN MCCULLOUGH, internet historian:

Troll culture. I would say that based on my experience as a kid on BBSes and newsgroups is I always expected . . . And now, again, I started going online at, like, age eight or whatever. And so maybe my expectation was that this was how adults behaved. But I always expected that people would be gross, but then I was also going online looking for porn. I remember finding and downloading *The Anarchist Cookbook* and things like that. So to me, one of the things that's interesting having lived through this is that I was inculcated very early on that if you go on a message board or a newsgroup, you're gonna encounter filth and people are gonna be mean to you. But then, at the time, you were doing something that no one else was doing. Your parents got you a computer and you're over there, they don't know what you're doing. So you're going on to be transgressive, anyway. And so that was part and parcel of it.

Looking back on it, I didn't expect things like that to go mainstream. I didn't expect my mom to be on the internet ever. I didn't expect her to be posting messages, commenting on blogs, and things like that. Now, if you had told me that it *was* gonna be something that everyone would do, I probably would have told you, "Well, it would mature and there'd be a way out of it." It's *never* changed. So, that expectation that there's people who are gonna be gross was there from day one for me. And then the problem is, is that now everyone's there, nothing's changed. It was fine when it was just dorky teenagers and total nerds trading porn and whatever else and cracked versions of *Doom* and things like that. That was fine, but the problem is, is that now all of society is there and it's still just as troll-y.

CHRIS MANCIL, EA global director of community:

Look, the reality is if you go back far enough to the hacker culture of people who had bulletin boards and way back in the day when the earliest stages of dial-up modems and the early beginnings of the internet and online culture, and certainly in some part of the nerd culture, there were certainly rebels in that culture. I mean, you certainly had engineers and scientists and you had some interesting enthusiasts like I would have been, and then there certainly was a darker side of people who are just trolls or hackers or people who were interested in stealing or just ruining things for others because it was fun and because you know what, these people aren't real. It is my contention that most of those people who were involved certainly in the late '80s and early '90s and late '90s were in large part gamers.

I think we built a stage and a platform for these people to come together. Twenty years ago, moderation was still kind of a new idea. Policing online communities was kind of a new idea. Banning people was a new idea. . . . I think that games do carry part of the responsibility of just being first to pioneer a new way for large numbers of people to play with each other in common spaces. And if you look at games like *Ultima Online* and *EverQuest*, they were very immersive, shared online societies that dealt with millions of people—certainly *World of Warcraft* later—and it brought together very diverse cultures that were devoid of some of the normal things that we would see in real life.

There wasn't a neighborhood, there wasn't society, there wasn't a government, there wasn't a culture. Actually, if anything, there weren't any social mores per se, other than codes of conduct and how to be nice to people. But the online space didn't have a lot of the things that we would consider when we made the social contract and came out of the wild and started living together as humans. I think we had to relearn how to enforce certain rules and codes of conduct, and we had to come up with police forces and customer support agents and investigation teams and community managers to make safe spaces and help people play nice and to resolve disagreements. I do think gaming, we're the victim of being first to have a lot of these problems on a bigger scale on the internet.

And also I think to some extent there was sort of a provincial, very backwards view at that time, too, that the internet was kind of ours. "Ours" meaning someone playing in Kentucky on the internet back twenty years ago didn't fully realize on an emotional level that the internet was global. I mean, a lot of people thought, "Hey, my neighborhood cable company just installed this and the only people that I know are close by." I think there was a sense back then that the internet was kind of like your local power company. It was, yeah, you're connecting to someone in San Francisco, but it wasn't international. And so I think there was a tendency to think of the internet as what we knew in our personal lives and not see it as sort of a platform for the world to connect. And that's something we see today and it seems obvious. But back then it certainly wasn't.

JONATHAN COULTON, musician:

When you talk about toxic videogame culture, I'm not sure you're really talking about videogames necessarily. [Laughs] I think what you're talking about is a smaller thread of this whole piece of rope called the internet and the way that we form into groups and the way that we interact with each other socially. [Laughs] I was just playing *Red Dead Redemption* and I'm all alone in my room and I'm playing it and I'm making some moral choices about whether or not to rob this person and whether or not to give money to this widow, but it's just me alone in my room and it's not a problem. The videogame is not doing anything to me. The toxicity that we're all feeling these days, I think doesn't come from videogames as much as it comes from people being in groups and interacting with each other online, and videogames are one of the many places that they do that. Certain games attract a certain kind of community around them. . . . It's not the screen that's causing the problem. I mean, think about what the content is and it's not even necessarily the content. It's the people around it.

In terms of a videogame culture and internet culture and nerd culture, I think the way things are set up, it has a tendency to amplify a lot of things that haven't been amplified before. There's this stereotypical image of an, I don't know, internet troll or a nasty gamer. [Laughs] Somebody who's alone in their basement with their dark thoughts and sending hatred out to everyone through various anonymous accounts online—and that's fine. That person doesn't do a lot of damage until they are suddenly able to connect with a community of like-minded people [who] start reinforcing each other's bad thoughts and bad behavior and start acting in a coordinated way and to start creating groups that exclude other groups and exclude other ideas. It's much easier for niche culture to get amplified, and that is good and bad.

I was very much the beneficiary of this particular effect of the internet. I had this niche-y thing: I wrote songs that were quirky and nerdy and spoke to a certain kind of person, and I never would have gotten anywhere if it weren't for the internet's ability to coalesce that community of like-minded people around this niche-y idea. Much to my dismay, over the last ten years it turns out that it doesn't just work for innocuous things like songs about monkeys and robots, but it works for bad ideas as well as good ideas. [Laughs] Hateful ideas.

RICHARD BARTLE, online game pioneer/researcher:

Well, the thing is that most people play games at the moment and "game culture," that's like saying "television culture" or "film culture," that's maybe a culture among people who are credible aficionados of particular kinds of games or game design or game music or something like that, but game culture? That which there is, is being put together by people who are not really representative of the people who are playing games. The thing is that lots of game designers and games researchers, they'll talk about "the players" as if that was a single unit: There is "the players" and this is what "the players" think, as if it was one person. But it's not. It's a whole range of individuals, most of whom are just the same as anybody else in real life. And some of whom, because there are some pretty bad people in real life, are pretty bad in games as well. It's just like the internet. I don't believe that games make people jerks, but they may attract people who are jerks. Unfortunately, there are so many of them.

IAN BOGOST, *Atlantic* writer/videogame developer:

What's the difference between [games and] any old deep obsession with a leisure activity, whether it's tennis or videogames or film or macramé or whatever? In the first case, I think a fair answer is that most people have a deep obsession or many deep obsessions in their lives, but those deep obsessions are not the defining traits of their character and their attention. You could be really into tennis or jogging and hang out with the tennis and jogging people on the tennis and jogging forums or wherever it is that they do that stuff. That's one aspect of your life, but it's not the whole of your life. You're not a jogger or whatever. Right? The fact that we have this word "gamer" is really indicative of this difference that there's just not a . . . We don't even have that word for, I guess we have "film buff," which just feels so quaint and it's a totally different thing. But it's the closest thing we have.

We certainly don't have it for books. You might refer to the book readers as a market category, but you wouldn't be like, "Hey, you a book reader?" That'd be a weird thing to ask someone. You'd be like,

"Well, I guess sometimes I read books." So that idea that the deep attention and the commitment to the activity is a defining character or personality trait, I think that's the first distinction. Also they might push off or push away all other knowledge or *most* other knowledge and experience. It would sort of feel like, "I don't need to do all this other stuff. I don't have a holistic, balanced set of interests." And that's something that I think all obsessions share with games.

What's the difference between a game obsession and social media obsession? In a lot of ways, there's no difference. The way that those communities can close in around themselves and make it seem as though there's no other world to occupy, even as there obviously is, feels very, very similar. The big difference really is that it's still much more socially acceptable to be obsessed with your physical appearance or with taking pictures of your clever lunches or whatever you can do on Instagram than it is to play *Fortnite* or whatever and have that be the activity that you're pursuing in lieu of all others.

BRIAN MCCULLOUGH, internet historian:
One of the greatest things of the internet from day one is also the thing that's killing it right now. Everybody's aha moment for the internet was when they went online and they found their people. If you're into alpaca farming or obscure bonsai trees, whatever, whatever, going on the web from 1993 on, everybody's first thing that got them onto the web was when they found their niche and these are my people and this is what I'm into. And that's what's great about the fucking internet, man. That's its greatest feature.

It's also its greatest bug because then like everything else, we just all scatter off into a million different bubbles and we're not even citizens in the same culture anymore. We're only citizens of the bubble that we create. And that could be ultimately a good thing. It's just that right now we don't know how to manage that and still live in a meatspace society together.

WAGNER JAMES AU, journalist/Second Life historian:
I got into Linden Labs and being an embedded journalist [in Second Life] and all that first by writing as a freelancer about games. I wrote about them for *Wired* and *Salon* back in its heyday. Actually, probably

the most-read article I've ever written is in 2001 when I was just starting out and I went to [videogame-industry trade event] E3 in LA. I'd been there before, but just that year over a bunch of others, it just seemed really, really cheesy. It was just a bunch of very dorky, socially retarded men-boys and it was mostly teens and early twenties. I called it the, uh, "industry for lost boys." It was really cheesy, booth babes and booth babes culture. Every industry has booth babes, or at least they're starting to get pushed out, but this was a game culture that seemed to be the only way the males were interacting with women was if they were part of the decoration or they're part of the game installation and so you can take photos and that was it.

It's still online. The title that my editor made was "Boobs and Rubes." [Laughs] My editor said that was one of the articles that got the most hate mail and I got hundreds of emails from mostly dudes just really pissed off. So when Gamergate happened, I was like, "Wow, this is so eerie that this is happening." But also that I didn't get anywhere near the amount of vituperation that the women involved got. I'm a dude, so it was mostly guys who say, "Fuck you, fuck you." You know, whatever. But I didn't get anyone like, "I'm gonna come over to your house and rape you and kill you." The dynamic was the same thing. It was male gamers who hadn't really thought much about their hobby feeling like they were being impinged upon by the outside and feeling really threatened. Even though I'm a gamer myself—and it should be clear in the article, I love games and I think they're important—but the fact that I was challenging their culture really enraged them.

ANGELINA BURNETT, *Halt and Catch Fire* writer:
Toxic fandom is just another phrase for tribalism. It is fundamentally human to find your tribe and protect that tribe. . . . Instead of connecting with the other fuckin' hunter-gatherers in your part of the savanna, you're connecting with people who are fans of Limp Bizkit. . . . It's *fundamentally* human. I don't think it's something that technology has gifted us. It's just who we fucking are.

STEVE JONES, internet researcher/professor:
Whether a community is healthy or toxic is never static. So, an example I'll give you is from some of my research where we're looking to

develop online peer-support groups for people trying to quit smoking. You can never guarantee that an online stop-smoking support group would not somehow flip so that, after a few weeks, everything charging along smoothly and then somebody in the community pipes up and says, "You know, I just can't deal. I have to have that cigarette today." The next person says, "That's okay. We all give in." And then somebody says, "Yeah, I think I may have to give in too." And before you know it, this support group to stop smoking turns into a support group that helps people start smoking again because they all say, "Well, you know, it's really hard. I can't do it. It's okay." Suddenly this group kind of does an about-face where it's supporting people who've been trying to quit smoking to take up smoking again because it's too hard to quit. So, no community is static and no community can of necessity maintain exactly the principles on which it might've been founded.

BEVERLY KEEL, Change the Conversation cofounder:
The internet is not making us be jerks. We're already jerks. It's just amplifying it. . . . I've been the subject of [a harassment campaign]. A local one. We had a candidate for national mayor who was a former Vanderbilt professor. She's a Black female who's ultraconservative and anti-Muslim, anti-immigration, anti–Black Lives Matter. This was now. This year. If you didn't know what she stood for, you would think, "Oh, she's an impressive progressive candidate."

And so I wrote something just on Facebook. I didn't take it to *The Tennessean*. I just wrote it on my personal Facebook page. The public could access it, and she posted it on her social media to enlist her people. I got vicious attacks from all over the nation. Somebody posted. I was called racist. I was called a cunt. Someone took my headshot and put a Nazi hat on top of it. And so, listen: I loved it because it proves my point.

I didn't [feel afraid] because most of the people who were threatening me didn't live here and they don't know her. It's just a political thing. But it could be very scary. Especially talking about toxic fandom, the hyper-fans are the crazy ones. And they're the kind of people who would show up at your door with a gun to defend the honor of their favorite celebrity. That's the power of the internet.

Ann Coulter and Rachel Maddow, both are beloved and reviled. And I'm sure they've both been called the same names. They've both been told they should die. To survive you have to be able to tune out the noise.

HOWARD RHEINGOLD, virtual community pioneer/writer:
The Chinese call it "human flesh search engine," when there's a bad actor. The famous Chinese case, and there were a couple of them, was this woman who uploaded a video [in 2006] of her killing a kitten with her high heels and that outraged people so much in China that they organized to find out who she was and harassed her. She lost her job and had to move. . . . Without the internet how are you gonna get a thousand people to harass somebody? It's much more difficult. Now, of course, it's developed into this unsavory culture.

DAVID WEINBERGER, *The Cluetrain Manifesto* coauthor:
From the very early days of the web there was the fat kid doing his lightsaber moves, a video that got passed around forever. Very low production values. It was 2002 and it was a kid in the garage. That got passed around because I assume people were making fun of him, and there's no particular reason to make fun of him. He was a kid who's practicing his lightsaber moves. [Laughs] That's embarrassing no matter who the kid is. But that was a very early example of something going viral and it was not a positive thing, the world passing around this poor, poor kid.

STEVE JONES, internet researcher/professor:
I can take it back to my PLATO days when people would stalk users. If they were on the network, they would see what terminal they were at, and that was usually highly gendered. It was almost always men stalking women, but it was to my knowledge—and that's an important qualifier 'cause there may have been other incidents—always one person stalking one other person.

I can also remember games where we would sort of play cat and mouse, where you would deliberately engage in a capture-the-flag kind of thing. You would have teams of people try to find players from the other team on-campus by seeing where they were logged in and sometimes you'd log in somewhere, but you knew nobody was in that lab so you can leave your log-in going. But that was a game. It wasn't with intent to harm. The stalking behavior, again, to my knowledge, didn't result in physical attacks. At least not here in U[niversity] of I[llinois] in Urbana-Champaign, but there's plenty of other campuses that had PLATO by the '70s and '80s that for all I know that might have resulted in sexual assault, but nothing on the scale of a Gamergate.

KUKHEE CHOO, media studies professor:

In 2005 there was a thing called "dog poop girl." A young lady was on the South Korean public subway train and she had her pet dog with her. The dog shat on the floor. [Laughs] The attitude—she was sitting in this indifferent, defiant attitude. And Koreans are pretty outspoken people, so I've no doubt that people were yelling at her, "Clean up your dog shit!" Probably she just ignored them and then she walked out. People were like, "Unforgivable! Unacceptable!"

She walked off and left the dog shit on the train and everybody just recorded or documented her or whatever they did. They posted her online and literally everybody online, whoever had the information, they start what the Koreans would call "they went to work." Basically the mob went and they literally shook the country. They found out what school she went to, they found her address, they posted it online. It was an *absolute* nightmare.

It's the online mob mentality at its worst. She was socially, basically, buried. There was *a lot* of talking after that. The society had to come to their own reckoning on whether that was acceptable or not. They weren't gamers, but they were the justice warriors online, right?

But if you really think about it, the people who went to work weren't the people on the train. They were the people who saw the posting and then they went to work. These are people just in front of their computer. It was like the entire country mobilized against her. It was *so* alarming. Of course, I mean, it wasn't the entire country. It's all these people online who were "doing their work." Doing investigation. They were having fun. It's basically mass bullying. Also, the fact that it was a young woman, it's not just about mob mentality: it was also a certain form of misogyny involved, which is similar to what you could describe with Gamergate.

REVA BASCH, Women on The WELL conference host:

There was a case, and this was in The WELL's Weird conference. I would just dip in occasionally when someone said, "Uh-oh, check out topic so-and-so." Weird was anything goes, and Weird was where the rules of civility that applied elsewhere on The WELL were suspended. Oh, good lord. What was the topic called exactly? Has [poet] Tom Mandel's name come up? Mandel, now deceased, had been deeply involved with another user, female user, and it was a bad breakup. I'm oversimplifying this in fact in part because I don't remember the details. [Laughs] And in part just because I'm pretty sure the topic is still there archived on The WELL. But basically, bad breakup, and [in 1992] he started a topic in Weird called "An Expedition into Nana's Cunt."

The idea being that here were all these people who were like, oh, gold miners or whatever, and they had their head lamps, then their pick axes and their backpacks and their whatever, and that they were exploring. Mandel was very clever and it was outrageous and horrible and so funny. I mean, it was just one of those . . . And I believe Nana left The WELL for a while at that point. So *clearly* it was just outrageous harassment of this woman.

And yet at the same time, given the ground rules of Weird, which were almost nonexistent, it was allowable and a lot of people participated. And a lot of people were shocked and horrified and going to the kind of meta conferences, the conferences about The WELL on The WELL and saying, "We've got to shut this down. We've gotta throw 'em off The WELL." And management, who I think were [The WELL cofounders] John Coate and Cliff Figallo, kind of went, "Mmm, it's never too late to do nothing at all." The Buddhist precept. They just kind of let it go. And I think there might've been a subsequent reincarnation years later of the same topic, but it was probably the best example—maybe the only example—I can come up with now of a kind of precedent for that systematic piling on or harassment that popped up or grew up in other parts of the internet.

HOWARD RHEINGOLD, virtual community pioneer/writer:

This brigading and online mobbing, vigilantism, is not gonna go away.

DAVID WEINBERGER, *The Cluetrain Manifesto* coauthor:

Let's imagine for a moment that there's always been examples of and sometimes persistent examples of internet asshattery, to give it too mild a term. This sort of thing, it goes back to PLATO and certainly for Usenet. I mean, there are examples of toxic Usenet boards. I can't remember which ones, but I remember famously: "Stay away from those." And The WELL as well, I think there were some cases of . . . Because in some ways The WELL was a gated community with utopian ideals, and it had to be heavily moderated.

So on the one hand, I think it would be interesting to point that out. On the other hand, I personally would want to not have the conclusion be that therefore the internet is evil. I think there are other conclusions, like people will tend to do this and public faces are moderated one way or another or designed one way or another.

So, the normal way in which I personally and my cohort are beaten up on this or takes the rap for it—which is, I think only partially true— is that a bunch of internet culture, web culture, was formed by web utopians who tended to be middle-class, educated white men who are very secure, who were aging hippies and saw this as a second chance to get some things right. And the idea was that you put people together in an open space and you let them do what they want and talk about what they want and in their own voices and magical things will happen. This led to a valorizing of unmoderated open-internet spaces, which works fine so long as it's a cohort of well-educated, middle-class white men who all agree on what's acceptable to them. But it doesn't work when you have the entire world which disagrees about what's acceptable and what works and what a good conversation is like and so forth and resulted in open spaces that were unguarded and thus were ripe for human infection and for effects that occur when you put people together in a place like that, assuming everybody is going to behave well according to your idea of behaving well. And so there is some truth to that.

I think Facebook . . . I've never met Zuckerberg. I think that he may even still believe that the right thing to do is to provide open spaces as free and open as possible and to let people be people and thus does not guard against the systemic infection of spaces by bad actors and for the magnified effects that a handful of assholes can have, or it can be more than a handful can have. I think there's some truth to that analysis and hypothesis. I don't think it's complete, but I think there is some truth to it.

HARRY DENHOLM, *No Man's Sky* senior programmer:

We're all feeling quite atomized. Did the sudden arrival of the internet being available and you can find groups of people who will reinforce your [opinions]? That's a pretty standard response, I know, but it's true. Joining forums in the old days where you'd hang out with people who are vaguely like-minded and who you could join [in] arguments against each other, the other side of the forum, pretty easily, you would feel at least you had your opinions were validated, because you had these virtual friends who believe the same way you did.

And I guess now, it's a lot easier to find those bubbles and insert yourself into them and feel completely valid by doing some pretty horrible shit because, you know, my mates are doing it. I have no idea what the life of your average teenager at school is these days, but if you are all incredibly well-connected via your smartphones and your social media system to each other and to the groups inside your school, you are almost being cultivated into bubbles from the second you get a smartphone basically. So you'll sort of learn that ability to think as a group and to maybe act as a group and to rationalize as a group.

Maybe that just becomes something that you learn very early on and so it just becomes more powerful as you grow older because it just becomes a natural thing. It's a well-worked-on muscle to be able to freak out on people because you know that you've got a group to back you up. No one is going and screaming at Rian Johnson for abhorrent SJW theming in *Star Wars* on their own. They know that when they do this, they're saying the right key phrases and they'll be there with their friends saying the same stuff. I don't imagine these people do it in isolation.

LISA NAKAMURA, gender and technology researcher:

I'm not a psychologist, but there's a term to describe when a behavior that's habitual is no longer permitted. It's some kind of extinction anxiety or something. I think that the continued outrage over *Ghost-busters* and *Star Wars* and *Ocean's 8* and Captain Marvel is going to be a woman and whatever it is can only go on for so long. [Laughs] Every time it comes up again, you're like, "Oh right, you guys again. Your picture franchise now has women in it." It just seems to be the dying gasp for some kind of white, masculine-centered idea about what's good.

CHUCK KLOSTERMAN, author/pop-culture essayist:

The [2016] *Ghostbusters* movie? I think that part of the reason people seemed so upset about that is because it did not seem in any context, to them at least, a natural freestanding event. It was perceived as being a conscious attempt to make a political statement about a preexisting entity that means something. It's just a bizarre thing. Thinking *Ghostbusters* is important is weird in any way. [Laughs] Like, if you care about *Ghostbusters* as a text, I think that's just weird, but that's what happened. If you say, like, "What can be done about this?," it's a complicated thing because to the people you're trying to persuade, it's probably going to have the opposite impact, at least initially. But it was just a *weird* thing. In a way, that's proof that these things are bigger than just the artifacts. The fact that anybody could care that much about *Ghostbusters* almost proves that the argument had nothing to do with *Ghostbusters*.

BEN FRITZ, *Wall Street Journal* bureau chief:

The culture of game fandom—it's pretty toxic, right? It's undeniable. There's a lot of toxic aspects of videogame fandom, which is not as true for movie fandom broadly speaking or TV fandom broadly speaking. Maybe because everyone's a movie fan, almost everyone's a TV fan? Only a certain portion of us are game fans.

That culture, unfortunately, among the outspoken elements of it are heavily male and there's a big misogynistic element to it. The internet and social media obviously fuel that often in the worst way possible. The loudest and most toxic voices get raised up and heard and then clearly that started to intersect with people who were upset about a female-led *Ghostbusters* remake and a female protagonist for *Star Wars* and perhaps even some stuff in our politics hold true, because online, those cultures have started to mix together. Misogynists find each other, frankly. I don't think it's fair to blame videogames, but there is the adjacent question of videogame fan culture, which has a lot of toxic and misogynistic elements to it. And why videogames have this big, big element to its fandom that is misogynistic is an important question. And unfortunately, I think the internet has made it so much worse.

KUKHEE CHOO, media studies professor:

What's happening in the States right now is quite interesting, right? It's like the pockets of all the political bubbles that we see all popping up throughout the United States seem to be an extension of what some people call toxic fandom, which I call toxic-internet culture. . . . They're scapegoating gaming culture. I don't think gaming culture is particularly unique. The way I see it is that they're scapegoating gaming culture like in the old days when they all blamed everything on the media. It's the same scapegoating.

So the people who are bashing *Ghostbusters*, that's actually just trolls. . . . I think it's a trolling culture that has manifested in this form. And I think Gamergate was also like that. These are not all gamers. These are the more core trollers within the gaming culture that did that. So I think that's one of the issues that should be separated. The gaming culture is not necessarily the trolling culture. But we see trolling culture everywhere and whenever the trolling culture emerges, you want to kind of blame it as, "Oh, that was the gamers doing that."

ANDRÉS PERTIERRA, r/AskHistorians moderator:

I grew up aware that [with] the internet, things can kind of blow up on you. Though over the last couple of years the line between people in different subcultures harassing you online and sharing stuff among themselves—which I've *always* known is an issue—and the more kind of like mobs and its connection to harassing people out of their jobs, that's more of a recent thing. I've always known that the internet could be weaponized by different groups, but it spilling over into the offline world seems a lot more common in recent years. Last five or six, I'd say.*

Back in the day? [Laughs] And back in the day isn't too long ago—we're talking about 2000—there was harassment, there was targeting, there was all sorts of stuff like that. But that famous Facebook photo of the girl who was taking the selfie and there was the poop in the toilet

---

* Interview conducted October 20, 2018.

in the background? I imagine she got a lot of crap from her friends and from people who are not her friends and that probably caused a lot of embarrassment, but I still don't know what her name was. I don't know where she went to school. I don't want to either. But you know, it's not like the lady who tweeted out the racist thing [in 2015] about "going to Africa, hope I don't get AIDS lol," and then gets on a plane and by the time she's off the plane she's been fired from her job. I don't remember her name now, but her name was everywhere. It was covered by the media.

I'm not saying these two things are exactly equivalent. My point is that harassment happened, but it didn't seem to create the geometrically multiplying degree of attention. The number of people who are in on it, the number of people who are aware of it, the fact that it enters popular consciousness, the fact that it can very easily have real world consequences—the lines between the internet and the non-internet have blurred over the last few years.

AMERICAN MCGEE, *Doom* designer:
I think perception has become distorted as a function of social media in a way that obviously—when I was making games, I started off, it was twenty-five years ago, 1993 or something, '94—we didn't have this sort of instant reactionary mob outrage. [Laughs] There was no function for that. There was no vehicle. The fastest you could get a game delivered to you was on the front of a magazine as a demo on a CD. Not even a DVD, but on a CD. So the speed at which outrage could spread and bubble over, it just wasn't there. It didn't exist. So I think partly what we're seeing is a function of the technology allowing for there to be such a thing as an outrage mob.

There's been plenty written and said on this topic of the psychology of social media being such that it feels like when I read something on Twitter, that person is standing right next to me screaming in my ears. That's the chemical, physiological, psychological equivalent to someone screaming in my ear that I'm bad or I'm wrong. And the way we react to that is as if someone was just standing right there. So we blow these things massively out of proportion and it's nothing to do with games, but it's just everything in life now has become as if someone is standing there screaming in your ear about it.

What's happened is that the point on it has become sharper because of social media, that the amount of outrage that can be generated and can be created and the amount of hate around a topic that can be created via these sort of faux media companies that build these hate-click articles around games. It's like a science now. It's like an art. They've figured out the absolute best way to go about manipulating a narrative to achieve the strongest results. And that's been an evolution. Ten years ago, no one was anywhere near as sophisticated with this type of stuff as they are now. But now it's like every one of these game websites is running a sort of psyops. [Laughs] They can use language in a way, weasel words, and suggestive descriptions to shape an image or a narrative out of *nothing*. And it's amazing to watch it day after day. And that's the thing, is any one of these things that happens these days would have been ten years ago a massive exposé that everyone talked about for weeks. But now we get one of those every couple of hours and it's already off our radar by the next time the next thing hits an hour later.

HARRY DENHOLM, *No Man's Sky* senior programmer:
    The one thing that I really saw and really learned through the whole *No Man's Sky** saga was if something is really popular and if something is guaranteed to generate clicks, then what is said about it is almost irrelevant. . . . So, there was a whole period of time where people were devising release dates for us because we were not releasing a release date. The conspiracies and the thoughts and plans and schemes were built up by people and then subscribed to by a bunch of other people, and then when they fell through, the anger would not be turned on each other, they will be turned upon us, which is a weird thing to experience. My experience with the internet up until actually joining and being part of this project was reasonably positive. Joining *No Man's*

---

* In 2016, criticism, heated debates, and negative reviews dominated the response to *No Man's Sky*, prompting Hello Games to address concerns and enhance the game through updates and patches that continue in 2024. The reaction arose from perceived over-promising of ambitious features before the game's launch. *No Man's Sky*'s promotion subsequently became a cautionary example in videogame marketing—and has likely influenced developers to become more cautious about disclosing too many details about their projects, fearing the repercussions of failing to fulfill promises.

Sky is when I've started to realize more personally that the internet can be used as a weapon.

The thing that I find hardest to talk about is probably the specifics of it. This I think would probably go for every game developer on earth. Not that I'm trying to speak for everyone. . . . During the time it was very useful to decompress by talking about some of the weirder stuff that was happening. Often they're almost, like, staring open-mouthed back at me, I guess? It sounds so ridiculous. Even looking back on some of it, I think it *is* ridiculous. I almost have to double-check: that definitely happened. Because if I just sat and read it, even myself, and I sat through it, like, it sounds so unbelievable. It would be a stupid made-up tale.

When I'm telling my mum like, "Yeah, there's this group of people who come and take pictures through our windows. And on Monday morning I go to work and I looked at our Reddit and someone had posted a picture of my desk and were discussing the quality of my headphones and the purpose of the champagne bottle that was placed near my desk and whether or not it was a celebration of our completion of the game and if that meant that the game is coming out at this date." It sounds like you're relaying an insane conspiracy theory, which is sort of exactly what is happening. But I think they're just like, "Oh, okay, that's pretty weird." I don't know if anyone knows how to deal with it, because I certainly didn't like it. It sounds ridiculous describing, because that's the thing that happened. But now I think back and I have no frame of reference to dealing with it either. We were all sort of just either putting up with it or just bottling in some of the insanity and just being like, "Okay, that's fine. That just happens now. That's just a thing we're going to get. We're going to get pictures of our desks on Reddit. Okay, we'll have to get some stuff for the windows."

JOI ITO, MIT Media Lab director:

I think that the forums and the bozos and the trolls of the early days, the worst they could do was ruin the mood of a room. But once you could take down websites, that was a whole other thing. And I think what's happening now in social media is you can actually destroy a person's online persona or actually literally threaten their lives, right? And like doxing and stuff like that. So I think that increasingly the online world's ability to direct something akin to physical harm at individuals has increased, and so the threat of toxicity to society has increased substantially. And we're putting more and more vulnerable stuff online as well. I remember when [hacker] Kevin Mitnick stole [journalist] John Markoff's email and posted it online [in the mid-'90s]. Well, it was kind of awful, but it wasn't the end of his life, but I think some people, if their email were posted online, it would be nearly the end of their life.

JONATHAN COULTON, musician:

Everything that's happening feels very evolutionary to me right now. And by that I mean here is this large complicated system—the internet, social media, blogs—and there are all these little bacteria floating around, all of us, floating around in this space. And occasionally some of us are gonna find the *very best* way to leverage this technology to do something and we don't really have any control over whether that thing is a good thing or a bad thing. But I think the fact that the nature of Gamergate and of 4chan culture and of the alt-right, men's-rights stuff that has grown out of it, I think, is an example of a brand-new kind of propaganda machine that is completely distributed. It's not anybody's master plan. It's just a thing that happened because people liked lookin' at pictures of cats with funny phrases on them.

CLIVE THOMPSON, *Wired* contributing editor:

I absolutely think there are things that Facebook and Twitter and Instagram and all the large social networks that emerged in the '00s could have observed [from online videogame communities]. They all were released with upbeat and naïve ideas about the value of merely connecting people: connecting people without there being any particular guidelines or rules for how people were going to behave towards each other and with very few protocols for dealing with abuse. So it's perfectly valid to ask, and I've talked to a lot of people who said, "Well, why were they that naïve?"

The answers that people often tell me are: "Well, they were a lot of young white dudes who had very little experience in their online world, direct personal experience of abuse, and so they simply didn't understand that *many* other cohorts of online users—women and people of color—very frequently get dumped on for saying even the most innocuous thing just because it's what they are." But it was probably clear at the time, and it's certainly clear with hindsight, that anyone building those companies in the early '00s had lots of examples to look backward to if they cared to look at history to see what types of bad behaviors can occur in online interactive environments.

And a couple of those examples were, frankly, just text-based BBSes in the '80s and '90s or blog forum posts from the late '90s and early '00s or multiplayer online games. All those games—*Ultima Online*, *EverQuest*, I guess even *World of Warcraft* was probably coming online a little around the time and maybe a little before a lot of those companies were getting big—you'd seen all sorts of forms of trolling and abuse happening on them.

Now, the interesting thing is of course, the games themselves? Those games often really didn't do much about it either, right? [Laughs] Like, they just let it happen and sort of said, "Well, this is thirteen-year-old boys being bad thirteen-year-old boys," without noticing that those boys were often being systemically terrible to women in a way that they weren't to other boys and driving women away from their games. So long as those games are making money, the people making the games didn't really care necessarily about this sort of thing.

RICHARD BARTLE, online game pioneer/researcher:
We [in games] knew all the stuff that was gonna happen and then it happened. . . . If you're creating something which is new, like Facebook, you're not going to think, "Well, this is very much like all these computer games that I don't play." Venture capitalists aren't going to say, "We'll put some money into this on condition that you speak to these guys here." *We* could recognize it, but if we're writing to Facebook saying, "Give us money to—No wait! Come back, please!" [Laughs] So, a lot of the things that happened were no surprise at all.

WAGNER JAMES AU, journalist/Second Life historian:
Can we have a platform that is basically a utopia? The short answer is no. The longer answer is you can create optimal communities that get us as close as possible to a golden-rule society or a content, optimal society. I've seen it happen.

DAVID KUSHNER, journalist/*Masters of Doom* author:

There's a lot of fucking idiots on the planet who don't have any-thing better to do, frankly. So, what are you going to do? That is the nature of the beast. I don't know that it's ever really going to change that much. You give people anonymity and power, they're gonna take advantage of it. We kind of have to develop new skills for how do we navigate this. What a lot of people choose to do is engage and what others choose to do is disengage.

I mean, you can go to a Philadelphia Eagles game and be sitting next to some belligerent drunk who's just completely obnoxious and yelling ridiculous things. You know what I mean? It's all kind of how you handle it. I mean, I don't mean to sound glib, but maybe I'm more of a fatalist. I don't think that we can change this. I think it's just the way it is. And I think people just got to figure out how they're gonna deal with it. I mean, because you don't want to deal with it too much. I mean, yes. Should Twitter ban hate groups and all of that? I mean, okay, there's an argument there, but there's always somewhere to go.

If you talk to young people about this, they don't even think much about it. It's so second nature navigating this and they often think that adults are just out of their mind, trying to understand why we're so overly concerned. It's like [the 1936 anti-drug propaganda film] *Reefer Madness*. I think that the reality is most people are able to figure this out for themselves, and then there's the ones that choose to engage.

There's always that kind of dichotomy or that tension between freedom of speech and then all the lunacy that ensues. It's not like that's new. You can go to Speakers' Corner in London and people stand on a box and say whatever they want. People can stand there and yell back or engage or walk by.

JASON MANNING, author/sociologist:

Are these things fixable? If by fixable you mean end conflict, no. [Laughs] You purge the most current load of the most outrageous jerks, and people will focus on the next level of things that caused them outrage and have to purge those and you'll just wind up with a purity spiral of eventually in the society of saints, the least saintly is the sinner.

ANGELINA BURNETT, *Halt and Catch Fire* **writer:**

There's a profound problem on Twitter, but there's a really easy way to solve this problem, and this is gonna sound glib and I will immediately follow it up with all the reasons it's problematic, but the way to solve that is to get the fuck off Twitter. And I understand that there's some people who the way their lives are set up and their livelihoods and their jobs, they do not have that luxury. I think there are way more people who do have that luxury than are willing to admit they have that luxury. I think we have a profound addiction to social media.

It's so far gone. I don't know how we turn the fucking tanker around. I feel like such a Luddite saying this, but the solution is to get the fuck off those platforms. It just is. At the very least, it's limiting your exposure and actively forcing yourself to go out and connect with community in-person. I don't enjoy knocking doors. I don't enjoy talking to strangers. I'm an introvert. I'm a writer. I like to stay in my house and make things up in my head. The act of canvassing and knocking on the door of a stranger and trying to draw out of them a conversation about what they care about, what matters to them? It's not fun for me, but it is life-changing and it is perspective-widening.

In 2012, I went to Ohio to knock doors [for political canvassing]. . . . It was so socioeconomically diverse. In the morning we'd be knocking doors on these million-dollar houses on a lake and by the evening I was nearly falling through rotting porches in the shadow of an abandoned rubber plant. I was walking through pee-stained stairwells in a housing project, then I was knocking doors on a little middle-class neighborhood with wreaths on the door. You can't ever go back from an experience like that. Within a compressed period of four days, talk to people from all fucking walks of life and you realize so quickly—I even sound like a fucking politician, but it's true—how much we have in common, how really all of us want is a comfortable life full of love and friends and family where we take care of each other. That's really all people fucking want and that's where the tribalism comes from because the center cannot hold. Once the community becomes billions of people, everything begins to collapse, and so your instinct is to make it small and protect it, but the reality is we all want that same fucking thing. And so when you can approach life with that perspective, all that other shit falls away. It becomes very hard to believe that a woman who said a racist thing before she got on a plane deserves to lose her job by the time she lands.

I don't know that the platforms can change. I don't know that there is anything that the platform can do, the way they're set up now, to solve this problem. We as individuals, as human beings, have to challenge ourselves to be better and we have plenty of evidence throughout history that that is totally possible and happens all the time, and we have evidence that we're totally fucking incapable of it and will fuck it up. [Laughs]

CHAPTER 9

INSTAGRAMMING WHILE
ROME BURNS

Assessing the Damage and Rekindling Hope

JONATHAN COULTON, musician:

The thing that I think about a lot in connection with the internet and this *huge* cultural transformation that has been happening and is gonna continue to happen is that we are the ghost in the machine. The internet is us. Granted, there are large corporations that filter it for us and serve it up to us in various ways and decide which tools we will be able to use to interact with it. But I think that's just one side of the coin, that we haven't yet figured out what the rules are on the internet.

It's a new kind of a social experience to be able to . . . I honestly don't know how many Twitter followers I have. It's more than a hundred thousand. But the idea that I can say something that a hundred thousand people might see? This is a brand-new idea that everybody now—even if you don't have a lot of followers—if you say something that gets outside your circle and goes viral, you may suddenly find yourself with an audience of hundreds of thousands of people or millions of people without intending that. And we don't know what that is. We don't know what that does to us and we don't know how to handle it. And we don't know how to handle it personally, just as humans. We don't really understand what it means.

It's very far removed from our biology and our evolution of just being monkeys living in groups. It's a thing that we haven't figured out how to regulate yet, and I don't mean regulation in terms of laws. I just mean in terms of norms and standards. That's obviously what companies like Twitter and Facebook are struggling with and many would say—me included—failing miserably at. It's their responsibility to start to help us figure out what these norms are. We just haven't evolved into this new thing.

Do you remember *Greatest American Hero*? [Laughs] You remember that television show? It's like we now have the superhero suit that came from space aliens and we don't have an instruction manual. It's great. We've got these superpowers, we're flying all over the place, but we don't know how to land! We keep crashing into stuff! [Laughs] We have so much power and we don't know what to do with it. And my hope is that it is so painful because we're figuring it out and that we eventually will. But that's only my *hope*.

BRIAN MCCULLOUGH, internet historian:

Things are moving too fast in terms of technology adoption. If you go online and Google for, like: How long did it take for radio to reach 90 percent penetration? How long did it take the telephone to reach— telephone being the perfect example—it *probably* took seventy years for the telephone to reach 90 percent penetration in homes in North America. So that's an entire generation of time for society to adapt. Social media and smartphones got 90 percent penetration in less than a decade. I think this is applicable to gaming, too, because things get adopted faster. What maybe is the problem *for so many things that we're dealing with right now* is that we just haven't had the time to work out the kinks in terms of the design but also figure out how to deal with it, figure out on the user end: How do I live my life now that this is in it?

It's a vague anxiety, but also they did a study, and baby boomers, one of the problems is if you take a thousand baby boomers and you show them stuff on social media, they can't tell what is an opinion from a fact. Versus if you have a thousand thirty-year-olds, they're better at telling, "Well, this person has posted something that's just their opinion versus this is written in stone and might as well be in the *New York Times*." That again speaks to the fact that if it took seventy years for social media to have been adopted, you would have had a generation that aged into it. You would have had given society enough time to figure this sort of stuff out.

Coming back to things like Gamergate, is it that we went literally from . . . Okay, I was playing Nintendo [offline] in 1988 and then by 1996 I'm starting to go on the internet and play *Doom* against people. And then five years after that you've got *World of Warcraft* and Second Life and stuff like that. Is that too fast? Is that too fast for people to culturally and intellectually or evolutionarily adapt?

I made this point once: So my grandmother was born in I think 1912, and so when you think of people like that, you're like, "Well, they went from airplanes to a man on the moon." But in her adult life, the only new technology that came into her home was the microwave because like, okay, TVs and washing machines and all that stuff? When she was an adult they were already coming in. She had radio, electricity, all that stuff. Think of that. Her entire adult life, the only thing that she had to learn how to use that was new was the microwave. Cars generally stayed the same. Airplanes generally stayed the same. TV, maybe the shows got racier or whatever and maybe you got more channels, but it was just fucking TV. The fact that tomorrow there could be some new social network or app that everybody has to get on and everyone has to learn, that can come literally overnight.

JON LEBKOWSKY, writer/early internet activist:
The early web or the early internet was pretty much like living in an area that's not heavily populated. . . . It wasn't mainstream, you know? The people who were actually online, they were kind of like pioneers in a sense. They had a pretty good sense of the technical infrastructure that they were in. A lot of the people who were online initially were actually technical people who work with technology on a regular basis, but not necessarily.

We're in kind of a real different world now than we were in then, partly because of the mainstreaming. You have so many people online now. And one thing that has evolved along with the internet has been this sense of silos and echo chambers, and people have been able to fractionalize culturally. I think you have a lot more of a potential for people to band together in a group that is a troll or a group that is hostile to certain kinds of things and to cause trouble. If they're technically proficient, you could have a group of people who really understand networks really well who do things like denial-of-service attacks. I've seen that happen and I've even been on the receiving end of something like that before. Sometimes it's playful and sometimes it's more toxic. Blissfully, I have not been in too many contexts where I've had to see stuff like that.

I can't think of any time in the early internet where we had the sense that there were gangs of people coming together to be unpleasant in some way. But I can imagine that happening now. I think that people can be manipulated to do that, too. You identify a set of people who have a particular emotional construct and you target them, you target them with messaging, and you give them the opportunity to connect with each other. You basically try to create a group thing where all the people are agreeing.

STEVE JONES, internet researcher/professor:

Echo chambers are just sort of a different manifestation of in-groups that perpetuate particular ideas among themselves. The scale and the speed are different [online] and the consequences are therefore different, but there is human nature. There is that need to find someplace where people seem to think like you do and then feel comfortable in those groups. So it's interesting to have kind of new terms like "echo chamber" and "filter bubble," but they're not really that different. They're not a particularly new phenomena, except for the scale and the speed. We've amplified what we've otherwise done in different spaces. Would a French salon in eighteenth-century Paris have been an echo chamber? What comes out of it would travel far, but it would take decades or a couple centuries. [Laughs]

AMERICAN MCGEE, *Doom* designer:

I think that what we see with games is there's a sense that the gamers, they tend to be fairly reactionary. They're a highly protective audience of their hobby. But what they do is they create, unfortunately, a perfect weapon to be used against the greater rights of expression by people on the internet. What's happened is we're slowly moving towards the lack of anonymity online. You've got to attach a real-world identification to your online account.

Well, that's exactly how it works here in China. And guess what they use that for here in China? They use that to make sure that you don't go say saying something that's not allowed by the party. I think gamers, by virtue of their closeness to the internet, by virtue of their passion for their hobby, they're being used against themselves and against us all to destroy a lot of the principles that made the internet and made the culture what it was back in the day. . . . You guys [in the United States] are living in a bizarro rage factory. Meanwhile, here in China, we're under the bubble of mass harmony. My house could be on fire, but I wouldn't know it because my access to the information is so effectively blocked.

From a fifty-thousand-foot view, my sense is that what we're witnessing online, on these social spaces, and if it's any relation to culture in general, these are all wedges. It's all somebody's form of marketing. When I say marketing, I mean influence or persuasion. My sense is that we have stumbled into a world where corporate technocrats—that would be the people who run Google and Facebook, Twitter—have an idea about the way to structure society and to manipulate control or otherwise influence people towards the types of behaviors that they think would best suit humanity.

ANGELINA BURNETT, *Halt and Catch Fire* writer:

In 2008 I worked on the Obama campaign and I shared an office—I was in Nevada—with the Nevada state digital director. His brother was one of the first Facebook employees. He was at Stanford. He built a company called Hustle. He's a low-key genius and he would be plugged into his computer coding *all day long.* And I love this guy and I think he's brilliant and he's definitely very soulful and he's recently sort of unplugged and stepped away from his company. He's traveling the world to try to get some perspective. But I saw just physically what you have to do to accomplish these technological goals. Just to build a simple app or a simple webpage, you have to go tunnel vision.

I don't think that's a healthy perspective when what you are building is going to *remake society.* I think that's really, really dangerous. So I don't morally fault Zuckerberg, for example. He was really good at a thing and he really loved that thing and he followed his passion. That's what in our sort of rugged individualist America, that's mythologically what we're supposed to do. But it's dangerous when what you're building will literally remake the world. It's really fucking dangerous.

I think pretty much as a rule in this country, we like to silo ourselves when it comes to the really high-powered professions. Medicine is also a great example. People go into a discipline and they narrow down. Once you get to a high level of medical school, you've often lost the concept of the entire body and how things are connected because you're a hand surgeon. I think the same is true with the development of technology. From what little I know of Jeff Bezos, the dude fucking, fucking loves his comic books. It's not like these folks don't read a book. I just don't think the educational pathways in this country force technologists to consider how technology fits within humanity, and technology *doesn't* come first. *We* come first. That's how it should work.

MOBY, musician:
I feel like we're just now starting to come up against the true cumulative consequences of our collective actions and people are slowly waking up and realizing like, "Oh, this might not work out." We're all like Nero fiddling while Rome burned. We're Instagramming while Rome burns. In some ways it's okay. We're taking pictures of it. We're sharing it. We're drawing attention to the problem. But we realize that politicians aren't the solution. More often than not they're the problem. Corporations aren't the solution. More often than not they're the problem. The clergy isn't certainly the solution. More often than not, it's complicit in the problem. So maybe this is necessary, and not to overreach with any of this, but maybe it's time for us to grow up and trust ourselves as individuals and stop assuming that the vested external powers have our best interests at heart, because there's *very* little to indicate that they do.

The way in which our emotional lives are governed by pixels and zeros and ones—I had this experience a couple of years ago. I don't know anything about professional sports and I was going on a date and I was going to pick up my date in Highland Park. And I had no idea, but it turns out it was Super Bowl night. And I didn't know this because I don't know anything about the Super Bowl. And I was walking through her neighborhood and because it's Los Angeles, a lot of people have their windows open. And I walked by a house and I heard these people screaming. I looked and I saw, like, ten people standing in front of a glowing box, screaming. And for a moment I saw it clearly and I was like, "Wow, isn't this odd that these humans, these complicated biological creatures, hand over their emotional lives to a screen? To pixels, flashing colors, and sound?"

We're so emotionally susceptible that *all* we do with our lives is let ourselves be hijacked by pixels. And sometimes that's pernicious in the form of racism, misogyny, bigotry. And sometimes it's quite beautiful. You know, like when someone is inspired by an image and responds with compassion. But also, again, from an ontological perspective, you take a step back and the subtext of our *entire* species at this point is semiotics relating to pixels—in both good and bad ways. But we tend to, in a qualitative way, look at the reactions that people have and we look at the real-world impact of pixels, but we don't ever really take a step back and say, "Yeah, but they're just pixels."

We live in a world that's falling apart, and people are distracting themselves pointlessly while the world is falling apart. I'd say the majority of what we call art and culture is time-wasting. Even if it's fun, even if it's nice—and I engage in it just as much as anybody—but the planet on which we live, the air that we breathe, the only environment we're capable of living in is being *seriously* compromised. And while this is going on, we distract ourselves with *Angry Birds*.

AMERICAN MCGEE, *Doom* **designer:**

I think this is the same thing where you hear people screaming about the hypocrisy of the control systems for content on platforms like YouTube. You've got tons of incredibly bad content that's in violation of YouTube's terms of service all over the platform, but they're only whacking the guys who are getting any sort of reach. So why don't we go and burn down their castle with our pitchforks and torches? I think it's all about division. And this is where the culture war as we understand it is actually—it's a war being waged *on us*, not *by us*. It is us being distracted from the reality of what's happening, the slowly boiling in the pot of water when we should be screaming about that. Not screaming at each other.

I think all of the outrage, all this stuff, it's a kind of wedge that's being used to slowly erode anyone's position to defend your basic rights to expression, to thought. And that ranges all the way from artistic expression and the types of games or television shows or whatever we create, all the way down to commentary expression by the people who consume those products: the gamers who are blamed for being entitled or insensitive when they reject a certain narrative or something that's being sold to them. And I think this type of thing we're seeing is happening across the spectrum of media and entertainment from news to games to music to comics. So that's my fifty-thousand-foot view.

And again, that comes back to my experience of being here in China and watching how they have a ministry of culture that defines what is and is not acceptable for consumption. How the Chinese method of controlling the population . . . Every day I watch the US getting closer and closer and closer back to like what they're doing here in China. Except in China, it's by virtue of a single-party government and in the US, it's by virtue of these mega-corporations that effectively control the means of communication and distribution of all thought and content.

I think people are missing just the scale of the kind of war that's being waged right now over the idea that the internet is a means of distributing media. There are a couple groups fighting for control of that right now, which would include Google, and then obviously is gonna include companies like Disney or Viacom or these larger media conglomerates who, many of them, they'd like to be in Google's position. They'd like to be the ones shaping the narrative. Of course a lot of these larger corporations do shape the narrative via their traditional media outlets like CNN or MSNBC. All of them are vying for control of the national narrative. And so from the outside, when I look back in what I see—it's almost like the US has become, in a giant format, like just watching Netflix. The absolute ridiculousness of the narratives that are being spun.

LORA KOLODNY, CNBC.com tech reporter:
Do I trust [the social media platforms]? They don't have a track record of being trustworthy. That doesn't mean they're not valuable.

I don't want to sound like . . . I'm very optimistic about tech. I think figuring it out is challenging. I think the volume of lawsuits companies and people sling at each other in the US complicates business here. It's one way people try to make money and it's complex and it's a reason I think these companies haven't taken greater responsibility because the second they step up, they're admitting liability.

I know I don't trust the platforms and I don't think the game companies are any better or closer. What can you do to limit somebody from sharing passages of *Mein Kampf* on a Discord chat room? I don't know. Nothing more than you could do about them sharing this on email. So the hope is more and better content comes into these platforms and to be interesting enough that it gets elevated above the hate-speech extremism and so on. . . . To me it speaks volumes when the platforms attempt to do something that seems responsible and it quickly falls apart, like Facebook had fact-checking initiatives with Snopes and that fell apart. I look forward to seeing if they can improve things, but I certainly think that the social media platforms have been under greater pressure than the gaming companies. And the game companies will lag and will follow the example of Google, YouTube, Facebook, Twitter, and even Reddit, which is still privately held and somewhat more okay.

I don't trust the platforms to algorithmically understand what's true and what's false, what's a decently reported story with reasonable sourcing, what is propaganda. I don't know that I trust them to understand what satire is algorithmically. You couldn't hire enough human moderators. So the answer for hate speech is more and better content. That would have to do with getting people who are educated to write and participate and speak up. But then you have this catch-22, right, where the women gamers don't feel welcomed to identify themselves as women gamers when they play and to speak up.

That said, I can't attribute it just to gaming. I think it's social media. I think it's punditry. I think a huge number of things led to it, but it certainly doesn't help to leave these things unchecked. I wanted to make that link because I've been a reporter for twenty years and I've never encountered the level of trolling that I have in the last few years.*

---

* Interview conducted April 13, 2019.

It's gotten to a fever pitch. I've covered Uber's first cease and desist. I broke a story about that and it used to be limited to the comments section, right? People wouldn't come after you face-to-face on Twitter or Facebook or by email. Now it's much more personal and it's much more hyperbolic and violent.

And I think that is inspired in part by the hyperbolic storylines and games and the trash talk that is encouraged in games in this repeated way that it's not when you have, like, a sports tournament or when you play an away game and you trash-talk with the other team there, you know, once a week. Games are *everyday all the time*, just like it is with social media. So that's what I think the effect is. I think it feeds into the decline in civil discourse. Gaming is not the only thing that's contributing to that. I wanna be careful to say my own industry is part of the problem with more opinionated blogging and punditry on-air and things like that.

And by the way, I'm pretty convinced that it's getting harder and harder for readers online and viewers online to understand what news even is, and that's by design. . . . People are trying to intimidate journalists out of doing their work. You know, people are trying to intimidate critics from doing a careful study instead of just an enthusiast blog post that's promotional.

RUKMINI PANDE, race and fandom researcher:

It is about what fits into narratives. My own work talks about the problems within female-dominated, queer-dominated spaces where the narrative has been that these spaces are great, they're progressive, they're subversive. And my whole shtick has been, well, maybe in some aspects, but they're pretty bad and continue to be. That's not something that is very popular as a take because it doesn't fit into the larger narrative about "good fans" and "bad fans."

So Gamergate . . . I think because, (A), it was people's jobs on the line, (B), because it directly affected an industry in a way that these conversations about shipping* and these other disagreements, I think

---

* Supporting or imagining various types of relationships, including romantic, platonic, or otherwise, between fictional characters from different media, often through fan fiction, fan art, or discussions.

they don't directly. . . . Gamergate was also kind of engaging in targeting advertisers and targeting journalism websites that were accompanying games, and I think that that heightened the visibility of the controversy.

Now more than ever we know that these communities are really transnational. We know that they have a lot of different people moving in and out of them. And while there seems to be evidence that certain parts of videogame fandom may well be engaged in toxic activities, that also overlaps into their online actions in other parts of their online lives. It's not as if it's happening *because* they're playing videogames. At least in my opinion, it's part of a larger problem with how identity issues within the US in particular are being articulated that is perhaps most obvious in those flare-ups. And so it becomes easier for people to blame people living in their parents' basement. [Laughs] It's lazy.

I'm not saying that there's no truth to the idea that a certain type of gamer might also be invested in whiteness or heterosexuality or any of those other kinds of majoritarian aspects of identity. But that doesn't mean that videogames are the only place that those ideas are being circulated. So it just lets everybody else off the hook, in a way. We are not talking about all the other aspects of videogame culture and videogame fandom. . . . I think it's too easy to just decide that that one section of fandom is the problem.

STEPHANIE HARVEY, *Counter-Strike* world champion:

I think our society overall changed in the last three years.* I think that right now we're trying to protect victims a lot more. We're trying to not let people get away with stuff, while before we were like hush-hush-hush. . . . I am very optimistic. I do think that things are changing. It's taking longer than I thought they would.

We're going at a pace that is, for me, not fast enough for the amount of things I'm learning—and I'm progressing as a human—but it's still moving forward. Like, a couple years ago, we would talk about, "Oh, what does it feel like to be a female gamer?" You know, we're way past that. Thankfully I don't have to talk about that anymore. [Laughs] I still have to, but it's very rare. It's more about, "What can we do now?"

---

* Interview conducted September 27, 2018.

VANGIE BEAL, *GameGirlz* **founder:**

I hate to say it. I hate to be that person that's like, "I did this twenty years ago and today . . . " I see no change. I really and truly . . . I've seen nothing happen in twenty years that makes me think things are different today. We've had these discussions for two decades. Change has not happened. And we know that change takes time, but really, it's been two decades. [Laughs] There's not really been a lot of change. And you will have game companies today that say, "Well, we've done this. *Hey*, we've taken the porn off the walls or we've added a system where you can report somebody." Really? Let's go to the women in the industry and let's go to the women gamers and ask them how that has impacted their enjoyment of their job and their hobby, because I think you're going to find it really hasn't.

I don't think you're going to have any game company that isn't receptive or that isn't going to listen to you. But do they actually take what you say and take your research, your reports, your opinions, and do they do anything with it? I would hope that there is some. And I think that just as time has gone by, even things like seeing more women working in the industry also creates a bit of change from inside the companies, and that of course is going to impact the products that they create and release.

[Sighs] Gaming is a business, right? No game company is really taking the lead here. I've not yet seen a game company say, "As a company that's been producing games for X number of years, we take responsibility and here's what we're going to do to try and make change." I don't think it would take many game companies all adopting that kind of forceful wall of "We're going to do something" for a change to happen. Unfortunately, I don't think that the people who are pushing for change—which is usually women groups and gamers—I don't think they're the ones that will ever make that change. As much as I have hatred for some of the stuff that happens, I confess I still buy games. It didn't stop me from supporting the companies, because it was my hobby and I love to do it. I still bought the games, even if I'm not comfortable with the people and the gamers sometimes.

I know that it does sound negative, but no, I don't see much change. I really don't. I can't even say that it's worse. It's just—it's the same. I don't see new issues today that I did not see when I did this. The issues are the same. The harassment is the same. The "throw under the bus because you're a woman" is the same. This has not changed. The people in the industry . . . I don't know. I think that it goes beyond gaming. It goes beyond gaming. It goes beyond technology. Women face harassment. It's no different in the games as how it is when you work at a grocery store. It doesn't matter what the industry is. These underlying issues are a part of the way life is today. It was the way life was twenty years ago. Changes in technology have suddenly made it easier for people who want to be harassers to connect with each other and create harassment on a large scale.

BRENDA LAUREL, Purple Moon cofounder:
More than a few powerful women in the industry have walked out the door and started and opened their own shops, and that's *great*, and eventually they'll hire some men. [Laughs] That would be great, too. I don't mean to put it all on gender, but it really is kind of all on gender right now. Gender and age—there's a tremendous ageism in the industry and VR as well. Tremendous ageism.

I talked to a friend yesterday who was working with a guy who was pitching an idea to some VCs [venture capitalists] for some interactive stuff. It's the third time he pitched it. He was pitching it to a VC who happened to be a friend and the guy was kind of sitting there looking neutral, and the person who was pitching saw this and said, "This will never get funded, will it? Is it because I'm old?" And the guy said, "Yeah, buddy, actually, to be honest, we don't fund people over fifty." [Sighs] So, wow. What got lost there was wisdom and experience. That scares me. There are a bunch of people like me and ten years younger than me who have trouble getting their nose in the door now because of our age. So that's a problem too. I think age diversity is pretty much as important as gender diversity in these cultural production organizations.

Social networks are taking so much heat right now, and it's because their sins are observable, quantifiable evidence. . . . So we can go after them because we have this clear, distinct idea of what they're doing wrong, and we can prove it. It's a different question with the game industry in the sense that you can't nail them on something that explicit.

I mean, if the employees of Electronic Arts or whatever—let's call it Blizzard, because I hate Blizzard—if the employees there get up on their hind legs like the employees at Google did, that would be a story. So the employees, say they walk out en masse because of the rampant sexism and the broken communication pathways and the general evil that their company is doing to the culture. They could do that and it would be in the news, so maybe one solution is trying to organize within game companies, the employees, to take a stand.

GRACE, *Fat, Ugly, or Slutty?* **cofounder:**

If it's still kind of normalized now—I mean, who is holding their feet to the fire right now? It's been up to the victims of Gamergate to handle it. You see various game developers just talk about that like, "Yeah, another day in the life of a game developer." Getting that level of vitriol for the level of entitlement that somebody thinks that they have over a particular intellectual property . . . I'm not sure that they've really been held to account for not standing up for the people in the community or even their own employees.

JENNIFER WADELLA, *Fat, Ugly, or Slutty?* **cofounder:**

I think things are better, because I feel like sharing a story in the first place takes a lot of confidence and guts to step up. If you've ever been harassed or sexually assaulted, it takes a lot of guts to step up and actually name that behavior and say this is unacceptable. And so I feel like we're seeing a lot more people step up. I think that's a sign of progress because there are a lot of dudes who just don't fucking know what it's like to live in our world and are having their eyes opened by us sharing these stories. So I think that's gotten a lot better, that more people are coming forward and saying, "Yeah, this is the norm."

KUKHEE CHOO, **media studies professor:**

Well, I mean, that's a similar question that people ask about the #MeToo movement, right? If you ask, "Do you think the #MeToo movement helped?" There's definitely more paranoid men out there and there's a stronger backlash at this point, right? There's always that pushback and there's that backlash but, at the same time, more women out there who feel encouraged to speak out. So there has been progress, and although the backlash might seem really strong now and some people might think that that's a setback . . . This goes back to the Hegelian dialectic. There's a thesis, antithesis, and then you come together: synthesis. Whenever there's a thesis and there's an antithesis and then there's a synthesis, that synthesis becomes a new thesis. And so it's kinda like a spiral. Hegel said that the spiral goes upwards to an ultimate utopia, towards God, towards the perfection. That's the positivism of Hegel. That's how I see it.

So, for example, the #MeToo movement is a thesis. Or you can do vice versa: patriarchy and sexism is a thesis. Antithesis is basically #MeToo, and then there's a new understanding, the synthesis. This new understanding is like, "Okay, we should treat women better." But then there's going to be that backlash of the incels and all those lobsters coming up. That's antithesis. Then you have to negotiate. I mean, this is how it goes. Every movement in history moves like this.

And in terms of the Gamergate, well, has it gotten better? People might not feel it viscerally, immediately, but ten years from now you look back you'll be like, "Oh, things got better." I was just teaching about racism, when slavery was abolished. I was just teaching about racism this week in my class. And one of my students was like, "Oh my God, holy cow, racism!" . . . I mean, they're only looking at those exceptions, right? I mean, seriously, that's what the problem is. History occurs when you write it, but the reality was it took *a hundred years* for Black students to be able to enroll in college. And so now we're not even, like, a hundred years. We're only seventy years after that. Not *even* seventy years. UT [the University of Texas] Austin actually accepted its first Black student in 1968. So, in that case it was only fifty years ago. So it's really, really amazing if you think about it.

The problem is internet culture has accelerated the sense of time. I don't know how astrophysics and everything works. You need to talk about Stephen Hawking in this case, like, time and space. It's your concept of time. Like, when you're running at the speed of light, everything seems to slow down, and that's how we're living our lives. Because the internet is so fast and instantaneous, all the changes seem *so freaking slow* but in reality much faster than it used to be.

BRENDA LAUREL, Purple Moon cofounder:
My belief is that everybody wants to heal, in the sense that every-body has a desire for their life to be whole. I think a lot of people are

unable to visualize what that means. A lot of that is the failure of education and the construction of communities. People get all uptight
and impermeable when they're stuck in the belief that they're getting
fucked and life is gonna be horrible for the rest of time and I feel bad
about it and I feel bad for myself. [Growls]

JASON MANNING, author/sociologist:
   This isn't something that I've studied personally, but I know some
tribal societies have very explicit rituals they use to try to cleanse someone who has committed severe deviance, like someone who maybe
has committed a killing might be banished for a time and then come
back, and they do a ritual. I think one of the Plains Indians groups did
this. They do a ritual where they basically cleanse the sin from the
group and from the person and, "Okay, you're back among us. We've
cleansed this and you're one of us again."
   It seems like something we lack, especially out in the online realm,
where you have people interacting who are just complete strangers and
anonymous to each other and you can get all that judgment without
any of the moderating influence of social closeness, of personal ties.
As far as I can tell, we've evolved no way of reintegrating somebody
who . . . Maybe they've learned their lesson, maybe they've apologized,
maybe they've changed their ways, but they kind of get banished to the
outer darkness until maybe eventually people forget about it. Maybe
that's our way? Maybe the cat chasing the tinfoil thing has an upside
to it? I don't know. Some way to bring about an ethic of "live and let
live" and try to get along? That's been the dream all along. It's hard to
maintain for any period of time, unfortunately.
   I think there's a lot of incentives now for holding onto grievances
and focusing on them. One of the things [my coauthor Bradley Campbell and I] talked about in [our book *The Rise of Victimhood Culture*] is
like, on campuses, [there are] a lot of cultural carrots and sticks for people to focus on words that have offended them, things that they think
have harmed them, and to advertise their status as somebody who's
been through a lot and deserves special consideration, demonizing
of privilege. Which means people who are accused of that then start
listing all the things they've had to deal with in a way to try to defuse
the accusation. So yeah, there's a dynamic of holding on to grievances

and focusing on the negative, which is not something I studied per se, but we do mention the work of Jonathan Haidt and Greg Lukianoff [figures in the fields of psychology and social commentary], who argue this is probably not mentally healthy, which I tend to agree [with] as somebody who's been through cognitive behavioral therapy. It's really the opposite of what they teach you.

It's also against a lot of wisdom of the ages: Buddha, Jesus, the stoic philosophers, Confucius, they all cautioned against reveling in your sense of how bad things are. This is a piece of it that ties into the online environment, which is these sorts of moral things, like starting a conflict or framing things in terms of a conflict, that seems to just be an effective way of getting attention, getting clicks, getting sales or whatever. People are moral creatures, tribal creatures at some level. There's a partisanship button in our brain you can push, I think, fairly easily for most of us. It's like putting sugar in the junk food. It's hacking the instincts to get some result. And so it's probably much easier to get attention and engagement and so forth by pointing to the negative.

We've known this with traditional media for years. If it bleeds, it leads, that kind of thing. This might just be another version of that in some way, but an even more conflict-oriented version where it's point at the bad person and say why they're bad and you'll get people jumping on to agree with you to show their support and take sides and be on the good side, the winning side, whatever. And since everybody's got a potential audience of people who would be inclined to side with them, everyone's got this incentive to hold onto their problems and focus on them and keep bringing them back up. That's how you get the retweets, that's how you get the hits. It's the negative reviews on YouTube that get all the likes and the views and that kind of thing.

STEVE JONES, internet researcher/professor:

We look through fog-covered glasses as much as we do rose-colored. So, to say that we're more fragmented now than ever implies a time when we were not very fragmented. I don't buy it. I don't deny the subjective feeling that things are shitty. I don't deny the longing for a time when they weren't, and things are qualitatively and quantitatively different now than they were before, but how much of it could be pinned on any one thing?

I'd like to think that if you take the long view here and you look at a long history, I think by and large things get better. That doesn't mean that things can't suck too. Look at #MeToo and you go, "Holy shit," but then you think, "Well, sometimes you've gotta go through this in order for things to get better." And you know, if we're going to go through this pain, it has to be in service of something. By and large in the history of this country, that's been the case. We tend to come through crises stronger.

AFTERWORD

The potential of what the internet is going to do to society,
both good and bad, is unimaginable. We're on the cusp of
something exhilarating and terrifying.

—DAVID BOWIE, *Newsnight*, 1999

THE TROUBLE WITH DISCUSSING OR WRITING about the internet is how little we all agree about what it is, and how unwilling we are to admit it. Is it a library? Shopping mall? Weapon? Real life? Data honeypot? Safe harbor for terrorists? Our only real hope for a better future? Simultaneously none and all of the above?

The internet isn't yet done revealing everything we're capable of making it out to be and into.

For example, in the 1999 interview with David Bowie quoted here, *Newsnight* presenter Jeremy Paxman shoots back: "It's just a tool, though, isn't it?"

Bowie responds, "No, it's an alien life-form."

The weird thing is that, while we have seen so much more of the internet since then, we still don't really understand it any better than Bowie or his skeptical interviewer. Twenty-five years after their exchange on the BBC, there's a growing belief about the internet worldwide that the old digital-age utopia we were all promised has curdled. Achieving any sort of constructive relationship with the internet today requires keeping it at arm's length. Casting a small shadow. Listening over broadcasting. You also must, in spite of everything, remember the internet's potential and that it's a perpetual work in progress. Forget about what the technology is doing now—think about that feeling you got from the first time you made virtual contact with someone in another part of the world, found a friend, and felt less alone.

When it comes to the online misogyny that Gamergate exposed, you can conclude that nothing really changed. Some corporations cooed—the Entertainment Software Association, the game industry lobby, waited three months, until October 2014, to break its silence with a statement that "threats of violence and harassment are wrong"—and then everything went back to business as usual. Which, unfortunately, is how these things go, as we've come to understand. After all, #MeToo didn't truly reshape Hollywood. Many who were "canceled" recognized the opportunity to just tap into a different audience. Why should this internet thing about videogames have a greater impact?

Or, you can conclude that Gamergate "won" because it recast buying and professionally criticizing a videogame as an act that is either moral or immoral—a binary right out of videogames like *Fable* or *Mass Effect*. Many videogame reviews now include disclaimers in fine print that the publication is "trustworthy," "unbiased," or "received a complimentary copy of this game." These statements are intended to assure readers that the critic has not been bought, inject more transparency into the professional relationships involved, and emphasize that the writer's opinion has not been paid for or influenced by the videogame company whose work they're covering. Gamers, like many other Americans, have long since abandoned the notion that journalists and critics operate with a certain level of integrity. It is not beyond their imagination that the $79.99 retail price of a videogame (coupled with the additional "perks" of writing about videogames, like junkets or swag like the by-default XXL T-shirts or branded lighters, pens, and bobbleheads) is enough to color or even sway a critic's review. Disclosures such as these are the last, feeble efforts to mend a frayed trust. Downstream, many gamers now take to comment threads and social media to increasingly imbue their preferences, loyalties, loves, and purchasing decisions with a kind of heightened morality—buying or liking one game is "bad," while not buying or disliking another game is "good." (Meanwhile, the compromised nature and symbiotic relationships inherent to games journalism haven't been scrutinized—YouTubers and streamers took the baton and now, with very little uproar, provide a foggy mix of news, opinions, entertainment, and branded content.)

Or, you can remember that before Gamergate, the escalating misogyny swirling around videogames was not really acknowledged.

Or, you can observe that nearly every single major American and Canadian videogame company with five hundred or more employees now has a diversity, equity, and inclusion lead or team. That was not the case in 2014 or 2015—one of several recent shifts that still feel surface-deep, though they can predate actual change, so long as the pressure remains. More broadly, there *are* now a greater number of prominent and observable non-cis white male voices in the industry. Ten years ago, trans game developers were largely invisible. Now you routinely see them in making-of documentaries. But across the industry's many awards ceremonies intended to recognize and celebrate its own creativity and talent—the Game Awards, Summer Games Fest, D.I.C.E. Awards, and BAFTA Game Awards—you can just as often see more diversity in the composition of presenters (though not winners, tellingly) as you don't. Gaming media now often calls out when this low bar has not been cleared.

The GDC's State of the Game Industry 2023 report surveyed 2,300 workers and found that 59 percent of respondents report a "moderate amount" or "great deal" of focus on DEI efforts at their studios, with 96 percent reporting these efforts were "at least slightly successful." Key initiatives include leadership commitment, staff investments in DEI recommendations, and mandatory training on DEI topics. But on the other hand, the report also reads "almost one-fourth (23 percent) of people in the industry are women and five percent are non-binary. The number of men (70 percent) in the industry remains the majority." The stance on player harassment toward workers included this response: "Accept it, let it go, move on. The loud minority is part of human nature."

But is all this awareness a reflection of cultural change from the outside, or a direct reaction to Gamergate? And how many of these companies sincerely recognize diversity not only as a bullet point in their next earnings forecast but something of genuine worth?

These big questions about Gamergate are impossible to answer because psychic pain can't be calculated. It's also cloudy because from early on and for the longest time, so many—critics, champions, and onlookers the algorithms invited along for the ride—were deer-in-headlights afraid, or busy rubbernecking, or assuming it'd all blow over, or just happily distracted by the novelty.

What's confidently offered from many pundits looking in the rear-view at Gamergate—and phonetically assembled as word salad by many gamers and workers in the industry—is to breezily conclude that Gamergate gave Donald Trump the cheat codes to becoming president via Steve Bannon's knowledge of *World of Warcraft*,* mutated into QAnon, destroyed democracy, and menacingly spilled into the real world when an internet-fueled mob invaded the US Capitol in January 2021.

I can't do that. But as you've already read, many of the people I've spoken to do hold this view—and that's fine. Our society has long been steeped in misogyny, racism, and xenophobia that it clearly has no appetite for confronting. That goes back a lot further than 2014—so does our appetite for answers. But in Gamergate, there is one coda that reveals at least some proof of how videogames and politics may or may not connect. In 2018, Brianna Wu, one of the movement's original targets, unsuccessfully ran for Congress in Massachusetts's Eighth Congressional District. She began a second campaign for the primary in 2020, but in April she announced her departure from the race, due to the COVID-19 lockdown preventing in-person campaigning.

What does this say about how videogames may or may not move and shape the rest of the world? Maybe just that Gamergate was a big thing within a community but overall went under the radar. But being right about these things, I think, is hard to get excited about. Like, the two-hundred-ton boulder we have to push up this hill we call America just got five pounds lighter, congrats.

---

* In 2005, Steve Bannon secured $60 million in funding for IGE, a company that employed low-wage Chinese workers to play *World of Warcraft* and earn in-game gold that was tradable for virtual items. IGE then sold the in-game gold to *WoW* players for real-world money. In 2017, Bannon—then White House chief strategist and senior counselor to the president—told Joshua Green, for his book *Devil's Bargain: Steve Bannon, Donald Trump, and the Storming of the Presidency*, that his role at IGE was how he had first become aware of and intrigued by gamer culture. Because *WoW*'s massive player-base forums were very active, fans could discuss strategies and meet friends, but they could also grouse about parts of the game they didn't like. Perhaps Bannon saw ways to leverage this discontent, because he said he was able to "activate that army. They come in through Gamergate or whatever and then get turned onto politics and Trump." Bannon claims to have tested these tactics while serving as executive chairman of *Breitbart News* from 2012 to 2016.

But I think theories like the Bannon–Gamergate connection are sort of autocomplete assumptions that get handed down and accepted as true due to sheer repetition. You can't prove them, but you also can't disprove them. They achieve escape velocity and have stuck thanks to decades of blaming videogames for so much for so long and video-games—basically—not giving a shit. Just because countless gamers had over the years grown too numb to respond to this blame (and lacked a sufficiently loud megaphone to offer rebuttals anyway) doesn't mean you can take the effect and make it the cause. We know, but can easily forget, that political processes and the rise of individual leaders are more complicated than that—and that you can't be simultaneously outraged *and* curious. Or, as one researcher-lecturer I interviewed summed up in more judgmental terms: "Anyone who talks with certainty about social movements is a charlatan."

All I know right now is, despite open-mindedly listening to so many people's conclusions and introspections on Gamergate for so long—and I started interviewing as soon as the movement began—I'm less sure than ever about anything. After nearly a decade of recording people's stories all over the world for six-hundred-plus hours, I'm mainly skeptical of anyone's ability to have any real certainty about Gamergate's legacy. It's still too blurry and too raw. But I can give you at least one likely obvious truism: the main thing Gamergate succeeded at was making people sick of thinking or talking about Gamergate.

I suppose you could count me as among them, despite the significant amount of my own—only—life I've invested in being on the other end of these conversations: Inviting people to share, simply to listen, and placing faith in the power of process over where we end up. Discussing where we are now, rather than always seeking solutions.

The truth might be that not enough time ever passes to really know anything. But just because I'm simply too close to it has nothing to do with the fact that a decade *is* a long enough chunk of time to start evaluating or reevaluating, depending on your familiarity, just what the fuck happened.

Everyone who just witnessed it was traumatized. People need time to process. After about five years, we go from fight/flight and get some distance. Ten years out, we start to lose all sense of causality/impact, but we can see more clearly than in the heat of it.

I'm just someone who watched things fall apart and wondered if they could be put back together in a better way. But I've never pretended to be someone who knew how.

Over the years, I've interviewed a few people for Don't Die who afterwards threatened over email to sue me if I published a word of our conversation, and I get it. (My guess is after we spoke, still curious about what we discussed, they Googled "Gamergate" and were shocked.) The desire to avoid personally pissing off the internet doesn't need any explanation. Self-preservation is a smart instinct to stick with, but in effect it further burdens the people already in the crosshairs, who never asked to be there, to do all the heavy lifting. It also denies the fact that, whether or not Gamergate is part of your lived reality around videogames or the internet today, whatever poisons it released are in the water now. Staying silent won't change that.

The price we've all paid is this cycle of constant anger and frustration that's flattened the way we talk to and view each other. It's everywhere. Gamers may have been early to bearing witness to this type of internet-inflicted trauma, but it's not up to videogames to "fix" society.

That's fine, because the videogame industry has plenty of fights in its own backyard. Big ones. As of this writing, videogame workers have begun to more forcefully find their voices since the pandemic—part of a trending clash between the people doing the work and the people demanding they go back to working in precisely the same way they did before. Workers in various sectors—such as fast-food, healthcare, and major retailers including Amazon, Target, Instacart, and Whole Foods—all reached their limits. Their strikes and walkouts were indicative of a collective unwillingness to go back to work with the same service-friendly smiles on their faces. Videogame workers also joined this wave, asserting their needs and concerns.

Public accusations of misconduct are becoming routine, and evidence of the industry's systemic failure to prevent harassment is becoming impossible to ignore. These problems are nothing new to anyone who has been even half paying attention to the rhythms and stage whispers of the industry—but this time, history has stopped repeating itself. Consequences aren't quite as rare as they once were.

In July 2021, a gender-bias lawsuit was filed by California regulators against Activision Blizzard, one of the biggest videogame companies, period, and publisher of some of the most popular titles around, including *Call of Duty* and *Overwatch*. The company has approximately 9,500 employees, who make games for more than 100 million players worldwide.

Among the suit's many revelations: Kerri Moynihan, a thirty-two-year-old finance manager at Activision Blizzard, died by suicide while on a company retreat in April 2017 with her male supervisor. A subsequent March 2022 wrongful death lawsuit filed by Moynihan's parents against Activision Blizzard alleged that sexual harassment was a "substantial factor" leading to her death. (The Moynihans' lawsuit mentions an incident that took place shortly before Kerri's death, in which "male co-workers passed around a picture of [her] vagina" at an Activision holiday party.) At company headquarters, the filing says, there was a "pervasive frat boy workplace culture . . . [where] male employees proudly come into work hungover" and contributed to a "breeding ground for harassment and discrimination against women." The July 2021 lawsuit, *California Department of Fair Employment and Housing v. Activision Blizzard*, points out that "unlike its customer-base of increasingly diverse players," women composed approximately only 20 percent of Activision Blizzard's employee population and endure "constant sexual harassment, unequal pay, and retaliation."

In the months after the 2021 lawsuit—which came after a two-year investigation—employees staged protests and walkouts, launched social media campaigns, and called for executives to resign. In a country with management-friendly labor laws, in an industry with hardly any union protections, an act of workers' defiance is no small thing.

Some Activision Blizzard executives did leave in the wake of the lawsuit, including J. Allen Brack, the head of subsidiary Blizzard Entertainment. The company pledged $250 million toward increasing employee diversity and promised to strengthen anti-harassment policies.

We can draw lines from Gamergate to all sorts of things but, boiled down, the movement was about misogyny, an open hostility against women for somehow ruining videogames, and people in positions of power not taking action. And in many ways, the brightest sign that we're starting the long process of making sure people understand that is not okay came in the fall of Activision's longtime CEO, Bobby Kotick.

Kotick had led the Santa Monica–based company since 1991 and, until these scandals, was the second highest-paid CEO in the S&P 500. In October 2021, he asked to have his salary and overall compensation reduced to the lowest possible amount under California law—$62,500—until changes could be made to improve Activision Blizzard's workplace culture. Before this, he had been making an average employee's entire yearly salary in a single hour.

Kotick told Activision Blizzard's board of directors that he hadn't known about the company's history of allegations of employee misconduct, which also included a woman who was allegedly raped by her supervisor in 2016 and 2017. But as the *Wall Street Journal* uncovered, Kotick not only knew about them but minimized and repeatedly hid his knowledge from the board. In a press release* issued by the now former CEO in October 2021—amid lawsuits from multiple government agencies—Kotick stated that his voluntary pay cut aimed to provide the company with "every available resource" to address its cultural issues. The release does not address his own role in fostering or overseeing these issues.

As all of this was happening, Microsoft set a deal to acquire Activision for $68.7 billion. After the deal closed in October 2023, Kotick announced he'd be stepping down on December 29 of that year. On December 15, Activision Blizzard and the Department of Fair Employment and Housing settled the lawsuit, with the videogame company agreeing to pay $54 million mostly associated with pay inequalities, but as stated by the Civil Rights Department, the settlement is based on no findings substantiating claims of widespread harassment within Activision Blizzard.

In 2016 and 2019, Meta's Sheryl Sandberg—who positioned herself as an advocate for women in the workplace with her 2013 book *Lean In* and her organization of the same name—reportedly, according to the *Wall Street Journal* in April 2022, leaned on the *Daily Mail*, a British tabloid, to kill stories about a restraining order filed against her former boyfriend: Kotick. The protective order had been filed by another ex-girlfriend who alleged that he had harassed her at home. If safety is a story, we also have

---

* "A Letter From CEO Bobby Kotick Regarding Progress and Commitments Made at Activision Blizzard," October 2021.

to realize—as Gamergate demonstrated—that we tell it to ourselves while navigating a world filled with people who want different things, people who understand that power can be used to deflect attention and blame to see what they can get away with for as long as possible. This is as true for gamers as it is for executives and advocates.

There weren't any articles written blaming Sandberg's or Kotick's alleged actions on videogames—just like there weren't any articles that blamed people who watched Miramax movies for Harvey Weinstein's acts—because we understand the limits and receding contexts for tired old arguments and excuses. If you wanted to be a pessimist, you could just notice and ruefully chuckle at all the ironies here, and then close the mental tab.

Or, if you want to live in a world that you hope is trending in better directions, you can remember that all causes are bigger than any individual—even those who behave one way in private and another in public.

As Kotick's downfall was playing out, Microsoft began its ritual cleansing to purge bad management and assure employees that they are in a far better environment. There are reasons to believe Microsoft will go the distance. After all, Microsoft has faced its own reckonings over the years, most recently in a 2015 class-action discrimination suit and in 2019, when employees protested its own "boys club" culture.

But as reasons to be optimistic about the future go, that's a pretty weak one. Corporations do nothing out of the kindness of their hearts. They don't even have hearts.

There's another story starting to poke out in these recent developments, one about the media. My mind flashes back to the 2020 documentary series *The Vow*. The HBO program takes a thorough look at NXIVM, a self-improvement group that turned out to be a cover organization for a sex-slavery sorority that blackmailed, starved, and physically branded its members into submission. But half of *The Vow* is about how nobody wanted to report on NXIVM. Again and again, we watch the documentary subjects call up members of the media to tell them that people are in harm's way, only to hear them say on speakerphone, "Well, we don't have a good time peg for it."

That also has been, for the longest time, the story of videogames. It's been a slow awakening, but per the mention of the *Wall Street Journal* here, this is starting to change. Even some of the most popular gaming enthusiast sites will now publish reports of worker issues at game companies.

It isn't journalism's responsibility to "fix" these problems, but their inattention—and the nature of media narratives and judgment calls in what's "juicy" enough to cover—certainly didn't help. While scandals at Activision Blizzard made the *Wall Street Journal*'s front page—at least online—incidents at other studios were at best below the fold or relegated to investigations by independent YouTubers. Incidents including, for example, the game publisher Annapurna Interactive being implicated in three separate cases of emotionally abusive management. And with Techland in Poland, it came out in a 2021 *TheGamer* report with ten anonymous current and former employees that "autocratic management, poor planning, and a toxic work culture that trickle[d] down from the top" were tanking morale and causing streams of employees to reach their breaking points, quit, and be replaced by others, whereupon the pattern would repeat. This situation was complicated by the fact that CEO Paweł Marchewka's wife, Aleksandra, is the company's head of HR. Most recently—and there will undoubtedly be others after this book has gone to print—French authorities in October 2023 arrested five former Ubisoft executives following an investigation into allegations of sexual harassment. The arrests coincided with a wave of departures and firings at the game publisher.

Things didn't get this way overnight. They were helped along by an incurious media. Business stories, financial dealings, moral panics, and market crashes competed for limited ink and real estate in magazines and newspapers. Videogame stories usually didn't make the cut. As one freelance journalist active in the '90s told me, "With the exception of Atari in the early '80s, I don't recall even knowing much about [videogame] worker issues until the very end of the '90s."

This means that by the time the internet went mainstream, videogame companies didn't offer much in the way of names and faces at all—unless you count Mario. Although online media operates without the print restrictions of column inches, no amount of sleeve-tugging could make editors interested in writing about the people at videogame companies. (Though, as one magazine editor working at the turn of the century told me over email, "Had someone approached me with a labor-related story idea, I would have looked into it. But no one did.") Articles about game workers and the realities of their day-to-days were too niche for more mainstream-facing publications and too much about not-games for fan publications. For close to a decade, my own reporting on these topics has run into these obstacles again and again.

I said in the beginning this book is not about me, but here's just a little about my typical experiences doing this work: In February 2016, a colleague referred me to a contact they had at *Mother Jones*, whom I proceeded to pitch via email on an article exploring gaming's need for unions, who forwarded that to another colleague, who a month later replied and suggested we find a time to just hop on a quick call and talk about my ideas, only for them to hang up on me the moment I said the word "videogames." I still have a hard time believing this really happened, but it did, and I never got an explanation. From 2015 to 2017, twenty-four publications rejected or lost interest in my proposals for meaningful journalism on the global workforce and creative field of videogames—many of which published similar reporting on periph-eral or parallel industries, like movies or visual effects. Eventually, I stopped keeping track. In 2021, one gatekeeper told me he felt that writing about "#MeToo topics" was "too backwards-looking." This is why, although I began Don't Die as a journalist, I now identify as an oral historian. The field of oral history more readily understands there are systems constructed all around us in which knowledge is marginalized, and all you have to do to fight against that is find some-one willing to talk.

Another reckoning will come when we're able to look into these stories and recognize how much tragedy, in and out of games, the media's fickleness has looked past. We're all navigating what account-ability looks like and media's role. But people understand media about as well as they understand Gamergate.

That the internet can sometimes cast an evil shadow is a known issue. What we're usually less willing to admit is, more often than not, when we talk about the internet we aren't really talking about the internet. We're talking about human nature and our worst impulses joining arms with technology, standing together to block out the light.

Steve Crocker, who was part of the late 1960s and early 1970s UCLA student team that developed the protocols for the ARPANET,* told me in an interview, after my work on this book was mostly winding down: "We're talking about things that are not specific or unique to the internet but endemic in the human condition. The fact that all of the issues that come up in every area of human life, from the most uplifting and thrilling creation of new ideas and building relationships and creating new commercial activities and opening up opportunities to the underside of it all—the bullying and the abuse and taking advantage of things—means that the internet has quite some time ago actually reached the point where it is a success."

I haven't withheld my opinions or judgments about Gamergate from this book because mainly—still to this day—all I have are questions. Division and siloing continue to accumulate compound interest. Someday the bill will come due.

Nobody got into playing or making videogames to look out for one another. Gamergate represented the first real schism where people who had opened their hearts to this pastime were asked to recognize they were complicit in some deep, nauseating problems. Like Trump or the COVID vaccine in the years to follow, Gamergate wasn't something you ever wanted to find out you held a different opinion on from the person you were talking to, because even passing contact with the "other" side instantly became viewed as a form of espionage—someone you thought you were on the same page with, it turns out, is on the "opposite" team. You unfollowed friends, separated from your body when dealing with coworkers or family. Disconnecting can become a way of survival, but it sure ain't a way to live.

We'll never know how many people got the final signal they needed from the movement and its fallout and realized, "Oh, I hate being in the games industry. I quit." Or, on the other extreme, how many people

---

* Designed to facilitate communication between research institutions, ARPANET (Advanced Research Projects Agency Network) was a predecessor to the contemporary internet. Ed Krol's *The Whole Internet User's Guide & Catalog* in 1992 described it as "an experimental network established in the '70s where the theories and software on which the Internet is based were tested. No longer in existence."

hunkered down and thought to themselves, "Yes, this is the hill worth dying on. I'm in."

Regardless of the numbers there, the reality is that everyone in 2024—in witnessing the further decline of ~~Twitter~~ X, the increasing awareness that Instagram and TikTok are hurting our youth, the begrudging admission that Google would rather sell ads than serve you good search results, and the coining of the word "enshittification"—caught up to what gamers have known since August 2014: something is wrong with the internet.

Today, Gamergate hangs in the air as an incomplete thought. A sentence fragment. Gamers stopped talking about it, nobody seemed to have been punished or called out in any major way, and many were just glad it somehow passed. We pretended it was a passing weather pattern, not the atmosphere we're all in.

If it wasn't too corny, I'd close by saying it's on us to start doing a far better job of listening to each other. To remind you that it's foundational to changing everything.

But in a way, it doesn't matter what I think about Gamergate. All I've ever really known is how to ask questions and listen. The rest, I leave up to you.

ACKNOWLEDGMENTS

THANK YOU TO EVERYONE who spoke to me and let me ask them a lot of questions that don't really have answers, trusting me to hear their stories in service of telling a bigger story about all of us.

I owe a big blanket thank-you to a ton of people who have been truly invaluable in offering ongoing moral support and a place to chew with my mouth open about all this complicated heaviness. The more I learn, the more I learn how much more there is to learn.

My deepest appreciation goes out to a ton of people who never turned away my many, many stray questions, requests for smell tests, and thinking things through out loud: Gus Mastrapa, Jen Carney, TK Shrodes, Jay Margalus, Jordan Raphael, Andrea Ayres, Ken Broholm, Tarn Adams, Gavin Craig, Ed Fries, Luis Hernandez, Tristan Donovan, Davis Cox, Gabe Durham, Erin Drake Kajioka, Tom Bissell, Paul Galloway, Reid McCarter, Tarn Adams, Jack Monahan, Steve Cook, Seth Langer, Zack Ellis, Troy Gaston, Rebecca Hiscott, Vernon Shaw, and Jen Cramer. Thanks to David Futrelle and Darren Wall.

Thank you thank you thank you to the following folks who either helped facilitate introductions to people or helped put people on my radar while doing the ongoing work of collecting as many perspectives as possible: John Szczepaniak, Drew Davidson, Henry Lowood, Patrick O'Keefe, Carol Benovic, Tim Seppala, Alison Tatlock, Jonathon Howard, Chris Kramer, Hugh Monahan, Aubrey Sitterson, Henry Jenkins, Carol Kirksey, Pippin Barr, Anne Jamison, Rosie Pringle, John Flansburgh, Mike Sacks, Len Kleinrock, Maura Conway, and Rosalind Wiseman.

While I spoke to a great deal of people, I had no way of knowing what I'd wind up using or not. So, although the things we discussed didn't wind up in print, they helped inform how everything was assembled in this book. A big thanks to the following for their time: Saru Jayaraman, Mark Stephen Meadows, Simon Cox, Alexandra Tweten, Ashley A. Woods, Matilde Park, Judy Wajcman, David Brin, Roane Edwards, Carly Kocurek, Mark Cousins, Alison Maclean, Margaret Heffernan, Lynn Walsh, Kyle Orland, and an anonymous early-internet user.

This book would not have been possible if it weren't for everyone I spoke to for and because of my interview series Don't Die (2014–present), where I continue to explore tangled questions about online culture wars, fandom, and labor issues in entertainment through the lens of videogame industry and culture. Those hundreds of individuals sharing their personal experiences and viewpoints have fueled my permanent curiosity about the questions that typically don't get asked.

I've also appreciated hearing from Don't Die readers, who have demonstrated to me that these interviews give people hope and feel less alone.

I couldn't close out thanks for Don't Die without also thanking Giles Copp for collaborating with me on the tech side with it and expressing my gratitude to Scott Gordon and Mark Riechers. Thanks to the faculty and students at the University of Washington's Information School, the Carnegie Mellon Human-Computer Interaction Institute, and Northeastern University.

Going further back, during the runway period before Don't Die, I'd like to thank Miguel Lopez, Evan Shamoon, and Aileen Viray for helping me nurture the seeds of where this all started.

Which brings me, finally, to today. A bonus thanks to Rebecca Hiscott—and Sid Orlando—who opened the door to working with Isabelle Bleecker and Jennifer Thompson at Nordlyset on this. We hit the ground running, and my head is *still* spinning as you continue to stay one step ahead of me.

From the bottom of my heart, thanks to Catherine Tung at Beacon. Your guidance, thoroughness, and "let me help you figure out how to say more of what you're saying" support in navigating the minefield that this book so obviously is have been both invaluable and incredibly meaningful. After a decade of living with other people's stories on this for so long, thanks for doing that for me.

To anyone else who I may have inadvertently forgotten—sorry, and thanks. I'm only (one) human.